KNOW MY VOICE SERIES

The Finger of God
ISRAEL, THE LINE IN THE SAND
PROPHECY - REALITY - SOVEREIGNTY
(Know My Voice IX)

by

Rev. Dr. John Diomede

To order additional copies of this book, contact:

Proisle Publishing Services LLC
39-67 58th Street, 1st floor
Woodside, NY 11377, USA
Phone: (+1 646-480-0129)
info@proislepublishing.com

My Sheep Know My Voice

My sheep listen to my voice; I know them, and they follow me. I give them eternal life, and they shall never perish; no one will snatch them out of my hand.[1]

Jesus (Yeshua) of Nazareth

But as many as received Him, to them He gave the right to become children of God, *even* to those who believe in His name, [13] who were born not of blood, nor of the will of the flesh, nor of the will of man, but of God.[2]

God said to Moses, "I AM WHO I AM." This is what you are to say to the Israelites: "I AM" has sent me to you.[3]

"As for me, this is my covenant with you: You will be the father of many nations. [5] No longer will you be called Abram; your name will be Abraham, for I have made you a father of many nations. [6] I will make you very fruitful; I will make nations of you, and kings will come from you.[4]

---

[1] John 10:27-28 MW
[2] John 1:12-13
[3] Exo 3:14 NIV
[4] Gen 17:4-6 NIV

Table of Contents

Preface

My previous writings have laid out in detail my journey with, and without, God. These writings have recorded the relationship that has become central to my life and existence. Hearing the voice of the Holy Spirit began to become both relational and revelational in my late twenties. Speaking for God has taken time, discipline, and focus. I have written ten books that all exemplify my understanding of hearing from the Holy Spirit and the considerations needed when speaking for God. Relationship with God, in a certain sense, is only a one-way street. God does not need to learn anything. We cannot offer God, universally, anything He does not have. God knows everything! The bible is the source and proof of this truth. The bible is basic and fundamental to all Truth. The bible is a revelation, and it is referred to as a revelation for this reason. It demonstrates that God is revealing to humankind the information we need to have a relationship with Him. The skin in the game for humanity, no pun intended, is our life. This relationship with God is not universal, it is individual. Our 'self' is the only item of value we can offer God, and it is a value that the bible says God desires[5]. Surprisingly this relationship is not very different concerning human-to-human bonds. Jesus' appearance on our scene two thousand years ago opened a new door to this relationship. God availed Himself to humankind in a personal, individual manner. This door does not change the bible. This door does not invalidate the bible. This door simply offers a personal experience through the voice and companionship of the Holy Spirit to all. This personal experience has several results that can occur within the individual as we begin to recognize truth[6]. First, it validates the bible. Secondly, it validates Israel's place in the plan of God as it relates to the entire history of humankind. Thirdly, it brings into perspective the organization-centric religion versus Holy Spirit-centric relationship. Fourthly, it brings a reckoning within the individual Citizen because meeting God, even in this manner, can have a profound effect on the life and

---

[5] The LORD your God is with you, the Mighty Warrior who saves. He will take great delight in you; in his love he will no longer rebuke you, but will rejoice over you with singing." (Zep 3:17 NIV)

[6] Jesus answered, "You say *correctly* that I am a king. For this I have been born, and for this I have come into the world, to bear witness to the truth. <u>Everyone who is of the truth hears My voice</u>." (Joh 18:37 NAS)

actions of a human being. For example, the realization of the status of oneself, and all humans, in the universe is solidified in the biblical principle known as the "fear of the Lord". This understanding becomes a guiding principle for life as opposed to an oppressive component of theology. Fifthly, it brings a humbling within the individual whereby they are now led by the principles of compassion and mercy in every aspect of their life (note that this humbling is more of an ongoing journey for humans that will be brought to completion upon their exit from this realm). Lastly, the person —and the idea— of Jesus, The Messiah, The King of the Jews, The King of the Universe, and The Son of God becomes the granite stone[7] of foundation in the life of the individual. This individual sees and hears the futile activities of self and humankind through a different lens as they journey daily through their days here in this realm. Their heart becomes overwhelmed with both the brokenness of mankind and the awesomeness of The Creator. These two realities combined yield one result. A sense of

---

[7] Simone Kefa (Peter) answered, "You are the Messiah, the Son of the living God.". Yeshua (Jesus) responded to him, "There is good for you, Shimon son of Yonah, because flesh and blood has not revealed this to you , but my Father who is in heaven........And on this **bedrock** I will build my community, and the power of Sheol will not prevail against it. (Mat 16:17-18MW)

humility, compassion, and mercy so strong that the individual is faced daily with the moment-by-moment awareness of examining their decision-making process concerning every action of their lives and every word that emerges from their lips. The question, "Who is on the throne of my life, me, or The King, Jesus?" must be answered. The principles embodied by this truth are biblical. The relationship is biblical. The witness of Jesus the Messiah is the Spirit of prophecy[8].

---

[8] And I fell at his feet to worship him. And he said to me, "Do not do that; I am a fellow servant of yours and your brethren who hold the testimony of Jesus; worship God. For the testimony of Jesus is the spirit of prophecy." (Rev 19:10 NAS)

Introduction

As I begin to write this book, Israel is currently in a physical war with Hamas, and a silent (and not so silent) war with many other nations and peoples. The Hamas war is what one would characterize as a real war, as war is defined. But Israel has also, and is also, fighting wars on financial, sociologic, political, religious, and cultural fronts. Yet, the most significant war Israel battles is spiritual. It has been going on for millennia. And the cause is not sourced in this realm. This is why they are the only people where their enemies embrace the concept of annihilation. There were other wars that seemed to lean toward this annihilation concept, but most allowed people to seek other places to live and did not "run down" their enemies for extinction.

Historically, this "extinction" principle[9], which has existed since Israel's beginning has not yet been eliminated or forgotten concerning Jews. Here in the United States, which is not the homeland of Jews, the idea and goal of killing Jews is alive and well. As I stated earlier, this concept crosses national borders, where

---

[9] "If it is pleasing to the king, let it be decreed that they (Jews) be destroyed, (Est 3:9 NAS)

Jews are concerned. This is what makes their hatred so unique. Everywhere Jewish people went, such as Russia, Germany, and many other countries across both the world and time, the hatred followed. What is so annoying about this tiny group of people that sets the world on fire, for millennia? The demonic beings of the spirit realm hate God. Israel has a certain place in God's plan for humanity. Since the source of this hatred is spiritual, their extinction would have spiritual consequences. Yet, the extinction of all Jewish people cannot occur because God will not allow it[10]. I will address this in more depth later in the book. And while the God of Israel is full of compassion and mercy this will change. Humanity's cup is filling up[11] with the anger and hatred that has become so normal in the lives of humankind. It is important to understand this is not a revelation for God, it is simply a matter of timing. So long ago The Finger of God acted by sanctifying Israel with His Word. That day long ago The Finger-of-God

---

[10] This is what the LORD says, he who appoints the sun to shine by day, who decrees the moon and stars to shine by night, who stirs up the sea so that its waves roar-- the LORD Almighty is his name: 36 "Only if these decrees vanish from my sight," declares the LORD, "will Israel ever cease being a nation before me." (Jer 31:35-36 NIV)

[11] In the fourth generation your descendants will come back here, for the sin of the Amorites has not yet reached its full measure." (Gen 15:16 NIV)

drew a line in the sand for all other nations to see! That line is Israel! There will come a time when an angry hateful humankind attempts to cross that line to extinguish the flame that is Israel. At that time God, as recorded in the bible, will intervene[12]. This will be a good time for Kingdom Citizens. It will not be such a good time for all who reject The King of Israel, for the Jew first[13] and then for the gentile. For Jewish people, and many non-Jews, God has taken too long to respond, but God, in His mercy is seeking all who might come over to Israel's side of the line to do so. Are you in that group? If you are interested in knowing more, keep reading. You may meet this God, The God, The Creator, The Judge, The King of the Jews, and Life Itself!

---

[12] Then the LORD will go out and fight against those nations, as he fights on a day of battle. ⁴ On that day his feet will stand on the Mount of Olives, east of Jerusalem, and the Mount of Olives will be split in two from east to west….. (Zec 14:3-4 NIV)

[13] ⁹ There will be trouble and distress for every human being who does evil: first for the Jew, then for the Gentile;¹⁰ but glory, honor and peace for everyone who does good: first for the Jew, then for the Gentile. (Rom 2:9-10 NIV)

Uncertainty and Prophecy

Humanity occupies an uncertain world. The circumstances in every area of life are filled with uncertainty. Humanity does not like uncertainty. Just follow the stock market. With uncertainty, it drops like a lead balloon. When the covid pandemic hit, pandemonium ensued not only in the financial world but in all areas of society. Day-to-day living, the hope of finding a companion, buying a home, having a child, making more money, seeing a loved one overcome a serious illness, growing a business and other positive expectations all turn on the hinge of uncertainty because humankind exists on the edge of a knife.

Humanity's existence is lived on the foundation of uncertainty. But God, through the bible and the people of Israel, offered a more stable foundation[14], Himself. The words of the bible, a historical account of the relationship of God and Israel and humankind, establish this foundation of certainty. The term the bible uses is prophecy. Prophecy has many uses aside

---

[14] 6 For in Scripture it says: "See, I lay a stone in Zion, a chosen and precious cornerstone, and the one who trusts in him will never be put to shame." (1Pe 2:6 NIV)

from telling the future. Its primary purpose is to establish truth. Truth can only be founded in God because God is Truth. Humankind, for millennia, has battled this fact[15]. But God, in His wisdom has offered humankind the cure for uncertainty. God offers His Word! Not only is that word recognized as biblical content, as it should, but the voice of the Holy Spirit has been given to us by Jesus and The Father. This Voice speaks truth. This Voice speaks God's word directly guiding those who would receive[16] guidance. God offers a solution to our uncertainty. Believe God's word and receive the Holy Spirit as a companion. Stand on a firm foundation and focus on the Voice that offers stability because the voices of the demonic and the world will have you wavering like a flag in the wind of uncertainty[17]. This truth is firm.

---

[15] 0 Above all, you must understand that no prophecy of Scripture came about by the prophet's own interpretation of things. 21 For prophecy never had its origin in the human will, but prophets, though human, spoke from God as they were carried along by the Holy Spirit. (2Pe 1:20-21 NIV)

[16] But when he, the Spirit of truth, comes, he will guide you into all the truth. (Joh 16:13 NIV)

[17] Then we will no longer be infants, tossed back and forth by the waves, and blown here and there by every wind of teaching and by the cunning and craftiness of people in their deceitful scheming. (Eph 4:14 NIV)

The Anatomy of God

Yes, God exists! This is certain, yet people have denied this fact. They are known as atheists. Other people have ignored this fact. They are known as agnostics. Still others who, oddly enough, have accepted the concept of God have spent much time fighting against God[18], mostly because they have issues with the concept of sovereignty. They are known as religious. These three groups occupy three arenas where they have hand-to-hand combat with God daily. Yes, God has a hand and an arm[19], at least. God offers us His spiritual anatomy not for His benefit, it is for our needs. It is offered to help our brokenness. It is offered for our understanding. It is out of mercy and grace that God allows this hand-to-hand struggle to take place[20]. Then there are times when God steps back from this struggle and humanity flails aimlessly punching at the air. Just watch the talk shows. When this occurs,

---

[18] 4 He fell to the ground and heard a voice say to him, "Saul, Saul, why do you persecute me?" (Act 9:4 NIV).

[19] 15 Remember that you were slaves in Egypt and that the LORD your God brought you out of there with a mighty hand and an outstretched arm. (Deu 5:15 NIV)

[20] 9 The Lord is not slow in keeping his promise, as some understand slowness. Instead he is patient with you, not wanting anyone to perish, but everyone to come to repentance. (2Pe 3:9 NIV)

human brokenness comes into full view. The symptoms are mostly seen in politics and the media. Hypocrisy, anger, and arrogance take a front seat. Arrogance is on full display. Humankind is not only broken but we are ill-informed. Unless God engages in the struggle, humility vacates the human psyche, and we are at a loss to understand that God's right hand can and has reached into this realm many times in very personal ways. God's finger reached into this realm[21] during the time of the prophet Daniel! God's arm reached into his realm during the time of both Moses and the prophet Elisha[22]. God completely reached into this realm as Jesus the Messiah. Today, the Holy Spirit reaches daily into our realm. God has done this over and over, but humanity fails to believe. And while I am speaking about hands and arms, one of the greatest pieces of evidence of our brokenness is, while we fail to believe in God, we embrace the belief that the demonic realm, who cannot affect our reality in physical ways, has the biceps to launch furniture, knives, and other objects

---

[21] 5 Suddenly the fingers of a human hand appeared and wrote on the plaster of the wall, near the lampstand in the royal palace. The king watched the hand as it wrote. (Dan 5:5 NIV)

[22] 17 And Elisha prayed, "Open his eyes, LORD, so that he may see." Then the LORD opened the servant's eyes, and he looked and saw the hills full of horses and chariots of fire all around Elisha. (2Ki 6:17 NIV)

across the room at human beings and rotate the human head three hundred and sixty degrees. This concept is often promoted by Hollywood movies depicting exorcism and is accepted as a fact by the masses. When will humanity learn? Since the resurrection of Jesus, God's voice, the Holy Spirit, affects us daily so we can be people of mercy and compassion. People who reject hate and anger. But only if we are willing to recognize and accept this help. God's voice can speak directly to us. We must listen, believe, and obey the voice of the Holy Spirit, the latest revelation of God's mighty hand and outstretched arm.

God's Voice and The Bible

When it comes to the bible, the idea of belief and faith is dynamic. Jesus told us this when he said the Holy Spirit would guide us[23]. Yet, people pick and choose from the messages of organizational leaders the information they want to believe and why they want to believe it without investigating the actual biblical material themselves[24]. What further complicates the problem is that religious groups create doctrine and dogma which interprets biblical content making the organization's messages replace biblical truths. These controversies are why we have thousands of denominations, sects, and religions and why there is so much uncertainty about this realm and the next. When religion speaks, God's voice is misunderstood and misdirected. Religious people don't like what I am saying. They want the relationship to occur between the organization and the individual so they can pay the rent. But Jesus said he would send the Holy Spirit to guide us. What does that mean?

---

[23] He will not speak on his own; he will speak only what he hears, and he will tell you what is yet to come. (Joh 16:13 NIV)

[24] Now the Berean Jews were of more noble character than those in Thessalonica, for they received the message with great eagerness and examined the Scriptures every day to see if what Paul said was true. (Act 17:11 NIV)

There is a unique relationship between the bible and the Holy Spirit, both being God's voice. The bible contains information fixed in time. The voice of the Holy Spirit is not fixed in time, it is dynamic. It flows with the world we live in and with everyone in that world—if they so choose. This is why Dietrich Bonhoeffer said the bible was a book you must inquire of[25]. If people choose not to embrace mercy, compassion, and kindness, they reject the principles that the Holy Spirit promulgates. And being a social justice warrior is not enough. God's mercy, compassion, and kindness differ from so-called "social justice" because to benefit one group usually means to exploit another. This is not true with God[26]. Rejecting Holy Spirit principles rejects the reality of God's realm, God's power, and God's sovereignty. The Bible says we must love mercy[27]! Human social justice loves selective causes. They only attach the idea of mercy.

---

[25] "You don't just read the Bible, you must inquire of it. Metaxas, Eric. Bonhoeffer: Pastor, Martyr, Prophet, Spy. Nashville: Thomas Nelson Publishing, 2010

[26] And we know that God causes <u>all things</u> to work together for good to those who love God, to those who are called according to *His* purpose. (Rom 8:28 NAS)

[27] And what does the LORD require of you? To act justly and to love mercy and to walk humbly with your God. (Mic 6:8 NIV)

Some would argue with me that the bible not only contains those good attributes but also contains anger, vengeance, and hate. I cannot deny that God declares there are things He hates[28]. I cannot deny God has anger[29]. I cannot deny God brings vengeance[30]. But Jesus dealt with and resolved the understanding of the how and the why behind the works of The Father. I call it wiggle room. Jesus also informed us why The Father gave us wiggle room in one verse[31]. God allows it because of our brokenness. And because authority and justice exist in The Father, our wiggle room was very expensive. Jesus paid the price for our wiggle room with his life. But The Father fully expects us to rise above our brokenness[32]. The Father sent Jesus to show how to rise above brokenness. Jesus walked the journey of humanity so that we may know it is better to choose

---

[28] You must not worship the LORD your God in their way, because in worshiping their gods, they do all kinds of detestable things the LORD hates. (Deu 12:31 NIV)

[29] And he passed in front of Moses, proclaiming, "The LORD, the LORD, the compassionate and gracious God, slow to anger, abounding in love and faithfulness, (Exo 34:6 NIV)

[30] Never take your own revenge, beloved, but leave room for the wrath *of God*, for it is written, "Vengeance is Mine, I will repay," says the Lord. (Rom 12:19 NAS)

[31] They said to Him, "Why then did Moses command to give her a certificate of divorce and send *her* away?" 8 He said to them, "Because of your hardness of heart, Moses permitted you to divorce your wives; (Mat 19:7-8 NAS)

[32] For the creation was subjected to futility, not of its own will, but because of Him who subjected it, in hope that the creation **itself** also will be set free from its slavery to corruption into the freedom of the glory of the children of God. (Rom 8:20-21 NAS)

God-directed humility than choose human-sourced brokenness. Historically, most of humankind has chosen brokenness which includes biblical misinterpretation of verses such as an eye for an eye[33]. The majority have chosen to live in self-denial of their own bad attitudes while vocally condemning others' bad attitudes. Humanity, at large, has chosen to live in a make-believe world.

---

[33] 38 "You have heard that it was said, 'An eye for an eye, and a tooth for a tooth.' 39 "But I say to you, do not resist him who is evil; but whoever slaps you on your right cheek, turn to him the other also. (Mat 5:38-39 NAS)

The Make Believe World of Humankind

Humanity has long sought out and followed soothsayers, oracles, psychics, fortune tellers, clairvoyants, and false prophets. They want to know what is going to happen, beginning with tomorrow, in the near and not-so-near future, culminating with the end of the world. The bible contains quite a bit of prophecy. Many would say validated prophecy. Much, if not all, biblical prophecy is defined by the Christian and Jewish communities. Some conclusions are very accurate, some uncertain, and some bring sharp discord. But both groups would probably agree that Biblical prophecy, as it is interpreted by each, is the essence of prophetic reality. The world at large does not adhere to biblical prophecy as accurately. In fact, they don't adhere to any biblical historical prophecies very closely. Secular society has built more of a prophetic patchwork consisting of what sounds good and fits into worldly philosophy. In the long run, humanity desires to live within the worldly mystical confines of Nostradamus's and the Ancient Incan Calendar. Society exists in a make-believe world. Let me explain. There is a movie, The American President. In this movie, the character of the president likens the practice of human acceptance of untruths to the drinking of sand to quench one's thirst when stranded in the desert. The idea of drinking sand when thirsty is preposterous. So is accepting untruths! But humans do it every day, as the movie portrayed – and it continues, just turn on any news or talk show. Human society travels on a trestle built of manipulation, misinformation, and lies. I have written in my previous books that we live in a world where talking heads on television can say anything that fits their narrative, true or not. And all sides have accumulated quite a following. They speak untruth and people believe. Humans drink sand because as the character in the movie says, "because they don't know the difference." They live in a make-believe world.

The conversation in the movie epitomizes the make-believe world of humanity. To what exactly am I referring? Humans are sand drinkers. Human beings follow the leanings of their specific leadership or talking head due to fear and arrogance. Human fear backs people into a corner of personal beliefs and arrogance lashes out like the tongue of a viper to defend this made-up information. Society is told the world will be ruined if the other group gains power! It occurs in every culture, religion, political party, club, school, job, it occurs everywhere. Those with the megaphone simply cannot see they are the culprits of the ruination. And this has been going on for a long time. It happened to Jesus[34]. The beliefs, opinions, and laws of the make-believe world sent him to the cross. The Father knows broken human rationale and he used it to send His Son to that cross[35] to secure our future. This life and this realm are temporary. There also exists a realm of life and truth apart from this temporary situation. Read my book, The Journey To The Next Realm, to find out more. Jesus of Nazareth gave his life for us to enter the Kingdom of God's reality, His Kingdom. It is not of this realm[36]. In Jesus' day, Rome held the power of this realm and much of the world drank Roman sand. So did political Jewish leaders, and some of the common Jewish people drank Roman sand also. For millennia,

---

[34]You do not realize that it is better for you that one man die for the people than that the whole nation perish." (Joh 11:50 NIV)

[35] Yet it was the LORD's will to crush him and cause him to suffer, and though the LORD makes his life an offering for sin, he will see his offspring and prolong his days, and the will of the LORD will prosper in his hand. (Isa 53:10 NIV)

[36] Jesus said, "My kingdom is not of this world. If it were, my servants would fight to prevent my arrest by the Jewish leaders. But now my kingdom is not from here." (Joh 18:36 NIV)

violence or the threat of violence, even for socially acceptable causes, was power. Why? Violence causes fear. Fear is power! But Jesus demonstrated real power by his resurrection. History points out what a debacle Rome's type of power was for people, so by the time Rome fell, humankind transitioned to the next make-believe environment. As time passed, laws of our civilized world that were intended to protect people were used to instill fear because they contained the power of legal penalties and were twisted to imprison the enemies of those in power. The South African Apartheid Government was a good example. That was another case of make-believe human decision-making made by people who were deceived into thinking they had power. And there were people who supported this atrocity, a fact of proof for my writings, fleeting human power, and the sand drinking mob. The battle shifted again when communication took front and center via television and now the internet.

As communications became more and more prevalent, it is the simplicity of words that ignites fear within each human. Today, the media and talk show hosts hold the power of this realm. The media daily releases articles and stories that instill fear. They have people drinking sand. If one party wins the election, you will lose everything. The threat is also repeated by the opposition. And these fabrications create the make-believe world in which humanity lives. People don't necessarily believe their group has the solution; they just believe the other is evil. Why? These untruths are simply tailored to the make-believe world of rhetoric. This is all designed by the voice of the demonic to keep you living in a make-believe world of fear and lies. The words are designed to affect your conscience by offering you the power to be the judge of good and evil, right, and wrong[37]. The leaders on both sides know most people have made up their minds already, they just need to feed that point of view with the daily dose of sand. The subsequent step in this make-believe world is to spread the lies with talk. People verbalize their judgments so others will think better of them. This verbalization makes the individual feel smarter and more important. But it is all anger and hate sourced in the demonic. Both sides level accusations tagging the opposition as racist, murderer or they are against

---

[37] For God knows that when you eat from it your eyes will be opened, and you will be like God, knowing good and evil." (Gen 3:5 NIV)

democracy, as if anyone knows exactly what that means because our democracy is make-believe. The entire media industry is built on this make-believe foundation. The saddest part of all is once you choose a side, the hate and anger are fueled by the opinions not only of the opposite side but your side as well. Unfortunately, it cannot be seen because the make-believe world is the only reality for the mob. One side of humanity hates and judges the other side as bad and evil while they blindly follow their make-believe rationales. This is not new. This make-believe structure has been alive and well for millennia. Jesus rejected the make-believe politics of his day[38]. Jesus rejected the make-believe religion of his day[39]. Jesus accepted and followed the principles of the real realm, which is communicated to humanity by the voice of the Holy Spirit. The realm of God exists, and you can take part of it right now. Jesus said his Kingdom was not of this world, yet he abided by its tenets of compassion and mercy while in this realm. His

---

[38] "Tell us therefore, what do You think? Is it lawful to give a poll-tax to Caesar, or not?" [18] But Jesus perceived their malice, and said, "Why are you testing Me, you hypocrites? (Mat 22:17-18 NAS)

[39] "Why do your disciples break the tradition of the elders? They don't wash their hands before they eat!" Jesus replied, "And why do you break the command of God for the sake of your tradition? (Mat 15:2-3 NIV)

voice, the voice of reality and truth, on which I will elaborate in a later chapter, speaks loudly, not through religion but through the voice of the Holy Spirit. This Voice calls to us every day. Don't let the make-believe world deceive you any longer. Become part of reality.

Hollywood

I like to be entertained. I am very appreciative of those talented individuals who bring to life the make-believe world of movies and television. It offers me a break from the stresses of life at times. My grandchildren also entertain me with their adolescent humor. They entertain me with their smiles and laughter. They entertain me with their drive to win a board game. They are funny. Interacting with them is the real world of relationships. But their interaction is based on our life together. They don't have some pretend agenda to get me to bend to their will, it is instantaneous, pure, and unabridged. It is real life; it is spiritual life. It is truthful innocent life that emanates from another source. Hollywood stories may appear like real life, but they are not voice of the Holy Spirit... The make-believe world of humanity, seeded by Hollywood, is the opposite of what I just described. It is manipulative, deceptive, and clouded with agenda-filled content. There is nothing spiritual about it because it lacks truth. Hollywood is a major driving force in our make-believe world. Let me offer an example. I watched a movie recently where the actor played a senior citizen who secured a new job after retirement. This character was perfect. He assisted all the younger employees with his wisdom, understanding, and support. You cannot help but desire to emulate this character. Within the confines of an agenda-filled movie, the actor did a great job. But the actor in real life has personality, social, and family problems, like me he is broken. This is not a put-down; it is a disconnect. And the disconnect is huge because unlike me, many people look up to him as a role model. Let me be clear, this hypocrisy occurs with both left and right, liberal and conservative, evil and religious. Hollywood makes movies full of political, social, financial, and religious manipulations with the primary goal of financial gain. In my last book about the deception within religion and Christianity, I put forth the concept that the voice of the Holy Spirit is muted by the voices of the demonic, the world, and the self. This confusion makes it difficult to divide evil from good, even if there is an appearance of good.[40] Hollywood is a seed daily sprouting branches that undergird the make-believe. Why does the make-believe exist? The inability of people to parse the four voices and focus on the voice

---

[40] And no wonder, for Satan himself masquerades as an angel of light. (2Co 11:14 NIV)

of the Holy Spirit feeds the make-believe world. This cyclical downward spiral is reinforced with the make-believe data we are fed daily. Jesus was mocked when he said his flesh was real food[41]. He appeared in the flesh and his presence offered daily data, food if you will, for the people's consumption. We consume the data, the flesh the world distributes daily and are ignorant of the process. You might ask, "is God in anything Hollywood offers"? The Holy Spirit can use anyone, any form of communication, any event, any message in any format. But keep in mind The Holy Spirit uses this data personally and individually to help the individual understand and recognize His voice. Let me offer another example. I like to watch the movie The Passion of the Christ at least once a year. I weep almost every time when the character of Jesus, while on the Via Dolorosa, says to the character of his mother, "I make all things new." The truth of the statement overwhelms me. But by the end of the movie, I am starkly reminded of the make-believe. The last scene of the movie portrays a naked Jesus, viewed from the side, walking out of the tomb after the stone is rolled away. Where in the world

---

[41] The Spirit gives life; the flesh counts for nothing. The words I have spoken to you--they are full of the Spirit and life. (Joh 6:63 NIV)

did they get the idea for this scene. It is not biblical, not godly, not true. Here is the biblical truth. The angel said to the women, who arrived at the tomb to continue the embalming process for Jesus' dead body, "Why have you come looking for the living where the dead are kept?"[42] Jesus exited the tomb before the stone was rolled away[43]. The moving of the stone was simply to reveal an empty tomb. Hollywood, in all genres, creates the make-believe. Humanity is becoming spiritually emaciated on this make-believe diet because it has no spiritual nutrition. It denies the existence of the hand of God actively working in our world. The voices of the world and of the demonic will always offer confusing, inaccurate, and divisive messages and claim they are the truth. Make-believe information believed by gullible broken people is deception. Only the power of the Holy Spirit can help you corral the distractions and lies and lock them off from negatively affecting your life. The filter of the Holy Spirit can not only help your journey,

---

[42] While they were wondering about this, suddenly two men in clothes that gleamed like lightning stood beside them...."Why do you look for the living among the dead? (Luk 24:4-5 NIV)

[43] an angel of the Lord came down from heaven and, going to the tomb, rolled back the stone and sat on it. (Mat 28:2 NIV) The angel said to the women, "Do not be afraid, for I know that you are looking for Jesus, who was crucified.He is not here; he has risen, just as he said..(Mat 28:5-6 NIV)

but it can help you have the courage to walk out your journey as Jesus walked out his journey.[44] with boldness.

---

[44] [1] He then began to teach them that the Son of Man must suffer many things and be rejected by the elders, the chief priests and the teachers of the law, and that he must be killed and after three days rise again. (Mar 8:31 NIV)

The Media

The internet as it exists today, and going forward, makes the media the single most powerful organization in the world. The arm of the demonic is always at odds with the arm of God but not in the way you may understand. The demonic urges humanity to achieve power and control. If you don't believe me, read the news. The arm of God, the Holy Spirit teaches self-control, along with love, joy, peace, patience, kindness, and gentleness[45] This may give the appearance that the demonic is more powerful than God. I assure you; they are not. What reinforces the demonic illusions? Although there are different media companies, they function on the same principles. One of those principles is arrogance. They would defend their stories and programs as informative, penetrating, and balanced. But there are obvious phrases that reveal this arrogance. One of these phrases is, "The truth is....." Truth is something very precious and not to be trifled with because its source is God's sovereignty. Yet, the crew of talking heads in the

---

[45] But the fruit of the Spirit is love, joy, peace, forbearance, kindness, goodness, faithfulness, [23] gentleness and self-control. Against such things there is no law. (Gal 5:22-23 NIV)

media will use these words to manipulate emotional responses and draw victims to their point of view. And do not be misled, they get paid to accomplish this task. What is so unconscionable about this methodology is they distort facts and rearrange them to build their own truth. Jesus exposed false truth[46] as invalidating God's word. This is a serious matter. Truth is reserved for ushering people to God, not to advance human political, religious, cultural, or social points of view. Any deceptive use of truth is arrogance.

The media's universal communication factor[47] offers a huge platform for the voice of the demonic and the voice of the world. I often reference the voice of the world so let me deepen your understanding of this voice. It reveals itself through the opinions of individuals who spout out the opinions of others. It is the mob. In the Garden of Eden, Eve was this representation. The voice of the world can come from a neighbor or a family member or a friend.

---

[46] or God said, 'Honor your father and mother,' and, 'He who speaks evil of father or mother, let him be put to death.' 5 "But you say, 'Whoever shall say to *his* father or mother, "Anything of mine you might have been helped by has been given *to God*," 6 he is not to honor his father or his mother.' And *thus* you invalidated the word of God for the sake of your tradition. 7 "You hypocrites, rightly did Isaiah prophesy of you, saying, 8 'This people honors Me with their lips, But their heart is far away from Me. (Mat 15:4-8 NAS)

[47] 6 The LORD said, "If as one people speaking the same language they have begun to do this, then nothing they plan to do will be impossible for them. (Gen 11:6 NIV)

The more notable worldly voices are the more public individuals such as actors, politicians, sports personalities, and talk show hosts. Media personalities are the biggest culprits that represent this voice because their voice summons the mob. The mob is made of people who want their fifteen minutes of fame and who now have a daily garbage dumpster to fill with their opinions, the internet!

In the world of media, there are two opposing sides. There exist liberal, progressive, and left-leaning, individuals, and then there are the conservative, status quo right-leaning individuals. Do either group speak for God? Many on the conservative side talk God. They write books on faith. They embrace long-standing family values. Does this make them purveyors of truth? The liberal side embraces non-standard values such as approval of gay and lesbian relationships, the agendas of the LGBQT+ and abortion on demand. Is this group purveyors of sin and antifamily values? The media includes both these groups and their representatives. But the deception is that neither are representing God. The media draw in their prey by appealing to their broken conscience encouraging the individual to be the determiner of good and evil. This is only a distraction to the more important issue, the sovereignty of God. Or otherwise known as the "who is in charge" dilemma. Who determines good and evil? God brought the flood that destroyed all but Noah and his family. Was God wrong? Was God evil? Sovereignty says no, but the talking heads of our time want to know if those who were destroyed were democrats or republicans before deciding. They have no problem stepping on God's sovereignty and claiming their "pride of life" sin[48]. Yes, there is a pandemic of human judgment that is alive and well on this earth, but all opinions are moot. The distraction is assuming that either of these sides represents or speaks for Jesus, the real Judge. Neither do! Consider this biblical message. Jesus said there would be people whom it would appear worked for him[49], yet The King will reject them. And then there is the opposite side who arrogantly boast of their authority to challenge even the idea of God. My point is both sides are selling deception. Both groups speak out of both sides of their mouth. Broken humanity cannot shake off

---

[48] For everything in the world--the lust of the flesh, the lust of the eyes, and the pride of life--comes not from the Father but from the world. (IJo 2:16 NIV)

[49] Many will say to me on that day, 'Lord, Lord, did we not prophesy in your name and in your name drive out demons and in your name perform many miracles?' 23 Then I will tell them plainly, 'I never knew you. Away from me, you evildoers!' (Mat 7:22-23 NIV)

its skin of hypocrisy. We have also been warned of this practice[50]. It is not my job to judge the media. I am simply pointing out the difference between hearing the voice of the Holy Spirit and the voice of the demonic. The media sells goods purchased from demonic thought and principles. It is the organization mentioned in the book of Revelation[51] whose leader opposes Jesus the Messiah. Their principles are division, hatred, anger, war, distrust, and the like. They oppose the voice of the Holy Spirit who teaches unity, mercy, compassion, and forgiveness. The voice of the Holy Spirit teaches us to lay down our weapons[52] of hate and anger. To use the power of our words and deeds for The Kingdom. This has never been and cannot be accomplished by an organization. It can only be achieved on an individual basis as each person communicates and has a relationship with the Holy Spirit. Currently, the hand of God allows all this to go on and has chosen the spiritual road to bring in His Children. This will not go on forever.

---

[50] Out of the same mouth come praise and cursing. My brothers and sisters, this should not be. [11] Can both fresh water and salt water flow from the same spring? (Jam 3:10-11 NIV)

[51] All inhabitants of the earth will worship the beast--all whose names have not been written in the Lamb's book of life, the Lamb who was slain from the creation of the world. (Rev 13:8 NIV)

[52] "Put your sword back in its place," Jesus said to him, "for all who draw the sword will die by the sword (Mat 26:52 NIV)

Politics

The bible speaks of two demonic leaders that will orchestrate the End Times events. They are known as the antichrist and the false prophet. The media, as spoken of in the last chapter, is the organization ultimately led by the false prophet. The United Nations and many of the Global conferences present some of the types of political organizations that support the appearance of the bible's antichrist. Eschatology, the study of the end times, is both intricate and complex. Many biblical messages are veiled or have dual historical timings. This writing is not on eschatology, it is on the fact that the God of the bible has a particular relationship with the Chosen people, the nation of Israel, and with all Kingdom Citizens through The Messiah Jesus. Since God does reveal eschatological events through the Jewish bible the revelation of these events is as real and substantial as is the existence of Israel. There is no doubt that End-time biblical events will culminate with the containment of demonic evil and the eternal security of Kingdom Citizens. But for now, we have the world of politics to examine.

Jesus said the demonic realm cannot win because it has no unity[53]. This probably stems from the fact that unity does not exist outside of the Unity of the Echad Godhead. Why? Because everything exists in God. Once a being, like Satan, chooses to challenge and reject God, they reject this necessity of existence. Humans, because of brokenness, lack unity. Look around and listen to the poison of politicians and media personalities all the way down to the anonymous comment maker at the end of every internet article. Combine the natural result of the demonic mindset with human disunity and the result is apparent, chaos. Only fear of reprisal from the government keeps most people in fear. And it is why politicians have no fear. Parts of society such as Portland, Los Angeles, New York, and San Francisco are already in a downward spiral. Why? The voice of the demonic is the source of mental illness. This combined with the voice of the world, such as Hollywood, the media, and politics removes all barriers to healing human brokenness. And just like the odds of winning a bet at a casino, the demonic forces will lose because

---

[53] Jesus called them over to him and began to speak to them in parables: "How can Satan drive out Satan? [24] If a kingdom is divided against itself, that kingdom cannot stand. [25] If a house is divided against itself, that house cannot stand. (Mar 3:23-25 NIV)

they require and rely on a broken disunified humanity to accomplish their goals. The result will be more chaos. Jesus was offering a prophetic perspective when he said this disunity will cause the failure of demonic forces because ultimately Jesus is the victory. How does all this fit in with politics?

Political leaders today cannot hide their hypocrisy. Some even flaunt this attribute. They roll from one side of an issue to another without the slightest bit of remorse. Vaccines for the Covid pandemic is just one example. They espouse hate for the other political party's members and, when convenient, hate for their own members. After the angry hateful comments of one day the next day they are standing shoulder to shoulder with the same individuals they derided the previous day. The voice of the Holy Spirit is deliberately muffled in the halls of every government building and the mind of every political official by demonic forces. The reason is simple. People are broken and broken people seek power, as did Satan[54]. So, they claw at one another to get to the front of the line in their make-believe world.

---

[54] 15 You were blameless in your ways from the day you were created till wickedness was found in you (Eze 28:15 NIV)

When a politician puts forth a position that appears to contain compassion and mercy it is only for the cameras. Political gain requires deception and a callous conscience[55]. Even those who begin the process with purity and innocence must succumb to the corruption of those powers which orchestrate this evil conglomerate or leave. If you disagree with me, consider Isaiah's charge against all humanity[56]. I have seen some politicians exit that environment voluntarily. The conscience can be a powerful force. I imagine they may have departed because it is difficult to stand in that sewage and hear their conscience or even the voice of the Holy Spirit calling daily to follow the guidance of God. But politics is usually a road to destruction.

---

[55] The Spirit clearly says that in later times some will abandon the faith and follow deceiving spirits and things taught by demons. 2 Such teachings come through hypocritical liars, whose consciences have been seared as with a hot iron. (1 Ti 4:1-2 NIV)

[56] All of us have become like one who is unclean, and all our righteous acts are like filthy rags; (Isa 64:6 NIV)

The Biblical Case Against Humanity

This chapter is mostly for people who say they believe what the bible says. The bible-believing, bible-toting committed blue bloods. There is a truth that we cannot escape. Humanity is broken and we are part of humanity so we must acknowledge that fact just as the prophets Daniel[57] and Isaiah[58] included themselves as part of broken Israel. We may not like this fact. We may not understand this fact. We may have trouble resolving this fact. But it is a fact.

There is another truth that we must face. The Bible not only makes statements, but the bible has rules. This presents a problem. One of these problematic rules is that the bible is infallible. Its content is infallible. It was directly given to its recorders from the Holy Spirit[59]. One of the favorite scriptures of the bible-toting community is found in Isaiah[60]. Isaiah, unlike me, was much

---

[57] While I was speaking and praying, confessing my sin and the sin of my people Israel and making my request to the LORD my God for his holy hill-- (Dan 9:20 NIV)

[58] "Woe to me!" I cried. "I am ruined! For I am a man of unclean lips, and I live among a people of unclean lips, and my eyes have seen the King, the LORD Almighty." (Isa 6:5 NIV)

[59] Ibid 16

[60] Ibid 56

bolder. He called all people sinners, which continues to emphasize the problematic nature of the bible! In attempting to keep an audience I have used the word broken to describe humans. And, in my defense, while it sounds different to the human ear, it does not sound different to the human conscience, spirit or heart of a Spirit filled Citizen. My brokenness reaches the depths of evil and is not for public consumption, it is a truth my inner being cannot deny. None of us would allow our thought life to be exposed! It is only the hand of God that nudges His children daily to listen and be obedient to the voice of the Holy Spirit. That voice of grace provided by Jesus comforts me so I can move forward for The Kingdom. Yes, my freewill plays a role but never does that role take on the deceptive thought that I am innocent. I am a sinner.

There are at least two additional biblical witnesses to human brokenness. Jesus, who feared no human, not only claimed we were sinners, but he took it a step further than Isaiah. He did this because he knew his sheep would hear the truth[61]. We know exactly how to

---

[61] For this I have been born, and for this I have come into the world, to bear witness to the truth. Everyone who is of the truth hears My voice." (Joh 18:37 NAS)

receive the words of our King. Jesus said we were evil[62]. You may not want to hear this truth. You may not like this truth. You may not understand this truth. You may not know what to do about this truth. But it is the truth. Only the voice of the Holy Spirit can instruct the individual on what to do about the weight[63] of their evil, we must interact with the Holy Spirit so God can break us out of our brokenness.

The second witness I want to mention is chapter eight of the Gospel of John. Jesus has an exchange with some individuals. The exchange is both complex and enlightening. The first twenty-nine verses contain mostly accusations from Jewish political leaders. After verse thirty it appears Jesus is speaking to people who seem to accept him but this also takes an alarming turn. When we get to verse forty-four Jesus says their father is the devil[64]. In verse forty-seven he goes a step further saying they are not of God. These are hard words

---

[62] "If you then, being evil, know how to give good gifts to your children, how much more shall your Father who is in heaven give what is good to those who ask Him! (Mat 7:11 NAS)

[63] "And he who falls on this stone will be broken to pieces; but on whomever it falls, it will scatter him like dust." (Mat 21:44 NAS)

[64] "You are of *your* father the devil, and you want to do the desires of your father...... "He who is of God hears the words of God; for this reason you do not hear *them*, because you are not of God." (Joh 8:44-47 NAS)

to hear, and religious people rationalize them all the time instead of allowing them to perform the work of God in changing the way they think and act. These words offer the cloak of humility directly from The King. They must be received because they demonstrate that biblical accuracy dictates one must be reborn to be of God[65].

These are biblical cases that stand in the face of human existence. The case is in the face of humanity because humanity has a history of hate, anger, and violence. Even under the guise of religion each of these symptoms have bubbled to the surface. The state of human nature should compel us to pay close attention to biblical information. And if biblical information is correct then we should be attentive to God's activity, relationship, and decision making, especially where Israel is concerned. It is only the voice of the Holy Spirit that can usher us into a reality where we must contend with the truth of God. This relationship can be both challenging and comforting but always leads to

---

[65]But as many as received Him, to them He gave the right to become children of God, *even* to those who believe in His name, 13 who were born not of blood, nor of the will of the flesh, nor of the will of man, but of God (Joh 1:12-13 NAS)

compassion and mercy, even when it is hard to perceive. I need to make one last point. God is not against us. The Father sending Jesus and the Holy Spirit reminds us that there is a biblical case "for" humanity. It is found in Romans 8:20[66]. God expresses hope for us. Knowing God has hope in us is the most encouraging message I have ever heard. It is like both of God's arms being wrapped around and hugging tight saying, "I believe in you"! Throw yourself on The King and allow him to break your brokenness.

---

[66] Ibid 33

The Working of the Holy Spirit

The problem with religion, and Christianity specifically, is they have a double standard. Christianity, at large, claims adherence to biblical standards and texts. Every denomination interprets those standards, creates dogma, and attempts to follow their principles. While their attachment to the bible rests on the fact that it was recorded by individuals moved by God the Holy Spirit[67], their interpretations nullify its content.

Today, many believe that the Holy Spirit is done speaking to people in the same manner as the Holy Spirit spoke to those biblical writers, unless you are in leadership, specifically their organizational leadership. But Jesus told us different. Jesus said the Holy Spirit would speak to us and lead us and live in us[68]. So why are we so dependent on men and women who claim they speak for God? Why do we exalt human beings? The more troubling question is why do leaders accept this

---

[67] Ibid 15
[68] Ibid 17

exaltation by other humans if they are truly of God[69]? Paul waited for credit from the only one who matters[70].

Those who disagree with me have said that my view would turn every book written by those who say they are led by the Holy Spirit into competition with the bible. What would make, for example, my book not equal to the bible? This is an important question to be addressed. There is no difference between the Holy Spirit speaking today and when the Holy Spirit spoke to Peter. It is the same Spirit of God. Peter and you, or whoever, are the same broken human representatives. It is the same! Most people don't realize that it was years after the resurrection when Paul rebuked Peter for separating Jews and Gentiles during meals[71]. Paul called it hypocrisy. Yet, Peter's letters made biblical content. Peter is not the problem. Peter was broken, just

---

[69] And I fell at his (the angel's) feet to worship him. And he said to me, "Do not do that; I am a fellow servant of yours and your brethren who hold the testimony of Jesus; worship God. For the testimony of Jesus is the spirit of prophecy." (Rev 19:10 NAS)

[70] I will get my crown I have fought the good fight, I have finished the race, I have kept the faith. 8 Now there is in store for me the crown of righteousness, which the Lord, the righteous Judge, will award to me on that day--and not only to me, but also to all who have longed for his appearing. (2Ti 4:7-8 NIV)

[71] But when Cephas came to Antioch, I opposed him to his face, because he stood condemned. 12 For prior to the coming of certain men from James, he used to eat with the Gentiles; but when they came, he *began* to withdraw and hold himself aloof, fearing the party of the circumcision. 13 And the rest of the Jews joined him in hypocrisy, (Gal 2:11-13 NAS)

like the rest of us. I believe God uses human messaging today just as God always did. But here is the key. The message is not from God because the writer claims it, it is from God when the hearer, in unity with the Holy Spirit, acknowledges it with their life of compassion, mercy and kindness. Because without the Holy Spirit-led faith the bible is just words[72]. There is a biblical flow to my claim. Let me share a metaphor of the process. The bible, both sections, establishes a flow of information. Let us call it The River of God. When teaching occurs, books are written or information is given, it must have been established in that River. The River establishes the source. All of the information that the Messianic Writings (the New Testament) offer was already in the current of the River found in Tanakh (The Old Testament). There is nothing new. But there is a problem, and you will not believe where it is located. What is rarely spoken of is that biblical translations contain distortions and manipulations. Compare the

---

[72] Because we all have heard the good news proclaimed to us, even as they did. But the word they heard did not profit them, because it was not joined with faith by those who heard.

following verses. One found in the NIV and the other found in The Messianic Writings.[73]

> [9] I know your afflictions and your poverty-- yet you are rich! I know about the slander of those who say they are Jews and are not, but are a synagogue of Satan. (Rev 2:9 NIV)

And

> I know your affliction, and poverty, but you are rich. And I know the blasphemy of those who declare themselves to be Jews yet they are not, but they are of an assembly of the Accuser. (Rev2:9 MW)

All of the bloviating done by Christian leadership about biblical accuracy is moot when they fail to recognize these obvious translational inaccuracies. Yet, God the Holy Spirit deals with this problem. The individuals who can hear the Holy Spirit research these and other verses. The voice of the Holy Spirit then can reveal the truth which occurs within the individual. This

---

[73] Gruber, Daniel. The Messianic Writings, Translated and Annotated by Daniel Gruber. Hanover: Elijah Publishing, 2011.

is how one's life begins to change. And you can bet your bottom dollar the revelation flows from The River. These individuals begin to fall on The Rock, Jesus. They experience inner transformation from the Holy Spirit. They are altered by this relationship. No longer is the voice of the demonic and the world veiled. It is seen for what it really is, angry, hateful, and manipulative. These individuals experience a life-changing, breaking, and God-sourced humility[74]. Before I wrote a word, this process had been going on in my life for fifteen years or longer. Today, words that I or others may offer, if they also are in The River, are inspired by the Holy Spirit. I have said it! These Sunday preachers are going to get up and speak for God without saying but they expect the hearer to know it. In both cases, the naysayers are too focused on who is doing the saying, not what is said. They should be more focused on learning to distinguish the four voices. Last week I read an article where an internet platform posted bible verses in slang that is common today among the youth. Some referred to it as blasphemy. The writer was focused on what was said biblically and translated it into slang. What if <u>what was</u>

---

[74] My sacrifice, O God, is a broken spirit; a broken and contrite heart you, God, will not despise. (Psa 51:17 NIV)

<u>read</u> brought someone to become a disciple of The King, Jesus? Once the Holy Spirit is involved, God can be trusted. Historically, the conclusions of organizational leadership concerning the interpretation of biblical text outweigh what the Holy Spirit may speak to someone. This should not be the case. A relation-centric life with the Holy Spirit always outweighs an organizational-centric membership. The testimony of Jesus is prophecy[75].

---

[75] Ibid 9

The Bible – Israel – The Nation – The Israel of God

The bible is not a Christian book, it is a Jewish book. It is a Jewish book that records the family history of Jews and other nations known as the gentiles. The fact of its Jewishness challenges almost everything we know or think we know about the bible. The first and most important factor on the journey to understanding this truth is to buy a book titled *The Messianic Writings* by Daniel Gruber[76]. You should also investigate his other writings[77]. The reason this is the first step is because all biblical translations have an agenda. This often comes as news to my readers. It is difficult to believe that translators tainted various verses. In the purest sense, some might believe that these translators simply had options due to the lack of existence of words and concepts from language to language. Whether out of translational options, ignorance, or intentional manipulation, the fact remains that the bible translations have been altered. I made this clear in the

---

[76] Ibid 73
[77] https://elijahnet.net/index.html

last chapter. Gruber's translation is an effort to translate from a Jewish perspective. To comprehend this fact reading his biblical notes is as important as reading the biblical text. Why is this important. For a few reasons. First and foremost is the concept of God's plan through The Messiah[78]. Second is the concept of God's plan for Israel. Third is the concept of God's plan for the gentiles. I will attempt to break down these three biblical thoughts.

The Jewish bible in the book of Genesis foretells of Eve's offspring. The bible uses the word seed[79]. This event and other connected biblical accounts regarding Abraham and his sons, recorded by Moses, indicated to Israel that there would be one individual (the seed) who interceded for their nation. One who was the Messiah (Messiah = The Anointed One). The life of Moses is a metaphoric example of this foretold individual. We know Moses was "like" the coming Messiah. Moses himself restates God's strategy in the book of Deuteronomy

---

[78] You Samaritans worship what you do not know; we worship what we do know, for salvation is from the Jews. (Joh 4:22 NIV)

[79] And I will put enmity Between you and the woman, And between your seed and her seed; He shall bruise you on the head, And you shall bruise him on the heel." (Gen 3:15 NAS)

when he foretells of the coming of "The Prophet"[80]. This theme is carried so strongly through the Tanakh (Jewish bible) that the idea of the Messiah, or The Anointed One, becomes common knowledge to all Israelites. Many historical mythologies contain a hero who can be likened to this Jewish Messiah, so what is the difference? The mythologies have many different heroes and gods. This Jewish saga has a single thread[81] running through millennia of history looking for this one single person. This information is referred to as prophecy. Over three hundred prophecies identifying one individual. This is the reason the choice of this individual cannot be haphazard. One does not tritely assign Messiahship to someone. And Moses' prediction in Deuteronomy is very specific. This Messiah would be a Jew, a normal Jew. Not unusually strong, such as Hercules. He would be virtually unrecognizable to the world. But to the biblical narrative, he would fit in perfectly[82]. Without the Jewish Tanakh, there is no

---

[80] "The LORD your God will raise up for you a prophet like me from among you, from your countrymen, you shall listen to him. (Deu 18:15 NAS)

[81] Diomede, John: *Know My Voice* I, The Mystery of the Thread of Israel. Proisle Publishing 2017

[82] Now when John in prison heard of the works of The Messiah, he sent *word* by his disciples, 3 and said to Him, "Are You the Expected One, or shall we look for someone else?" (Mat 11:2-3 NAS)

Messiah, and gentiles would still be looking to the likes of Zeus and Mount Olympus.

Now about Israel. For millennia, the world has attempted to shove destructive non-Jewish principles down the throats of Jewish people. In our world, culture destruction has become an offense to all except the destruction of the Jewish culture. This is not new, read the biblical book of Esther. But Israel still stands. And Israel will continue to stand[83]. The Finger of God has drawn a line in the sand and just like the ocean has boundaries so, the gentile world cannot cross this line in their efforts to destroy Israel. <u>Israel's existence is God's line in the sand</u>. What I refer to here is the nation of Israel, the people, the family. Since the grandson of Abraham, Jacob, or as God renamed him Israel, this people group has contained obedient individuals who called on their God and individuals who did not[84]. Yes, Israelites are the Chosen people but not all follow the God who chose them. Many non-Jews have attempted to use apostate portions of Israel to invalidate Chosen

---

[83] Ibid 11

[84] 6 Moreover, Manasseh shed very much innocent blood until he had filled Jerusalem from one end to another; besides his sin with which he made Judah sin, in doing evil in the sight of the LORD. (2Ki 21:16 NAS)

People status but, it is not about the people, it <u>is about the One who did the choosing</u>. So, the wheel-spinning of these detractors is futile. Concerning those Israelites, or Jews, who make their god not the God of the bible, their destiny, like all of us, lies in the hands of the King of Israel, The Messiah. The Bible also contains prophecy concerning this group and claims only a remnant[85] of Israel will remain, but Israel will remain, forever! So, the line in the sand is drawn, this line is Israel. Israel is this earthly nation consisting of those who choose the God of the bible, the prophecies of Tanakh and The Messiah, The King of the Jews, and those who do not.

Then there is the Israel of God[86]. The Israel of God is a group promised to Abraham. God told Abraham that all nations would be reconciled in him[87], in his seed. This word seed takes us all the way back to Genesis and Eve. This seed was Jesus of Nazareth. He was born a Jew and revealed himself to Israel. He was crucified with the words "King of the Jews" hung over

---

[85] For though your people, O Israel, may be like the sand of the sea, *Only* a remnant within them will return; (Isa 10:22 NAS)

[86] 6 And those who will walk by this rule, peace and mercy *be* upon them, and upon the Israel of God. (Gal 6:16 NAS)

[87] Ibid 5

his head. The Jewish politicians did not like it[88]. The Messiah is part of the thread of Israel, and He is The Thread of Israel! Read my book, Know My Voice I, The Mystery of The Thread of Israel. Jesus also stated that he would bring in other sheep, gentiles[89]. Isaiah also said this Messiah would be a light to the gentiles and these nations would place their hope in this Jewish Messiah[90]. Jesus, the Jewish Messiah patiently waits for The Father's timing[91] to return and restore all that was promised to Abraham's offspring and community known as Israel. The understanding of these promises is found in the bible and via the direct voice of the Holy Spirit. The promises encompass both Jews and Gentiles. These are the prophecies of God revealed by His voice, the Holy Spirit.

---

[88] And so the chief priests of the Jews were saying to Pilate, "Do not write, 'The King of the Jews'; but that He said, 'I am King of the Jews.'" 22 Pilate answered, "What I have written I have written." (Joh 19:21-22 NAS)

[89] 16 "And I have other sheep, which are not of this fold; I must bring them also, and they shall hear My voice; and they shall become one flock *with* one shepherd. (Joh 10:16 NAS)

[90] He says, "It is too small a thing that You should be My Servant To raise up the tribes of Jacob, and to restore the preserved ones of Israel; I will also make You a light of the nations So that My salvation may reach to the end of the earth." (Isa 49:6 NAS)

[91] He said to them, "It is not for you to know times or epochs which the Father has fixed by His own authority; (Act 1:7 NAS)

An Indictment of Christian Thinking

As I was growing up the three forbidden topics at get-togethers were sex, politics, and religion. I never really grasped the challenge until well into my fifties. What did that philosophy yield for us and our children? We left sex to the pornographers. We left politics to the wolves. We left religion to the wolves in sheep's clothing. And there they stayed. For this reason, there was, and is, a general lack of zeal in religious social circles to accurately resolve biblical thought. One of the symptoms was we rarely prayed before meals unless we had company or were at a party. After all, we weren't heathens!

Now that we all live in a world filled with words, even for those of us who are dumb, we see people publicly acting religiously for various reasons. There is situational protocol, religiosity, or fear of sounding stupid if we ever decide to pray. But where God is concerned, boy, have we missed the mark. And the saddest part is we are missing it for those we love most. Recently a relative said to me they never want anything to come between us. It was a curious comment. It was not necessarily a timely comment, as our relationship is fine. I believe it was a position-establishing comment. Long ago, my faith and their religion parted ways. Many family members I know would never leave their church. I espoused reasons for this mindset in my last three books. The Holy Spirit kept bringing their comment back to me for a week. As far as we understand love, we love each other and our family. We both probably believe we would never do anything to hurt our family. The question is: what will hurt our family? Switching churches or missing God? Does church membership provide eternal security? You may have heard the phrase, "You believe what you believe, and I'll believe what I'll believe." This is where Christian mainline denominations are failing people.

Jesus loves all. Some of his life, when examined, presents some real problems. He was challenging. He was knowledgeable. He was fiercely protective of those close to him. He was directly confrontational, especially to the Jewish political leaders. And most importantly, Jesus said he came to bring a sword[92]. Jesus

---

[92] Do not think that I came to bring peace on the earth; I did not come to bring peace, but a sword. 35 "For I came to set a man against his father, and a daughter against her mother, and a daughter-in-law against her mother-in-law;

established The Father's position, and anyone who wants to hold onto an organization more than the Messiah directly challenges the Messiah, not me. My position is established in The Messiah.

Organizational adherents are confused. They desire their church more than they desire The King, Jesus. Why? Because The King brings the sword! He brought it to my life! My journey goes beyond the border of their definition of Christianity because his sword has circumcised my misdirected heart. When one fears organizational ostracization more than The King, they can only apply their religiosity within the borders of their organizational understanding. They want to be the ones sitting on the throne of their life. They want to be the lord of their life. This choice only leads to being a lord of flies.

The above scenario has made Christianity problematic for me. Christianity represents many people who submit to organizational biblical teaching

---

[36] and a man's enemies will be the members of his household. [37] "He who loves father or mother more than Me is not worthy of Me; and he who loves son or daughter more than Me is not worthy of Me. [38] "And he who does not take his cross and follow after Me is not worthy of Me.

[39] "He who has found his life shall lose it, and he who has lost his life for My sake shall find it. (Mat 10:34-39 NAS)

rather than Holy Spirit biblical teaching. If Christianity claims to represent Jesus, the central figure of the bible as its leader, the inconsistencies are challenging to anyone who makes a true critical assessment of the religion. Let me offer an example of this challenge. Who, or what, represents real Christianity? This is a real dilemma that few people are willing to take on. Many cultures exhibit the same problem. In the Italian culture, one can find politicians, artists, sculptors, cooks, stone workers, and criminals. They are all referred to as Italians. But which ones do we want to represent the Italian culture? The problem is that attempting to identify the national culture from these individuals has resulted in, to say the least, confusion. The movie *The Godfather* is a perfect example. Many Italians idolized the movie for its cultural depictions. Vito Corleone had good intentions. He helped widows. His entire family was murdered by evil men. He was not such a bad guy. Just as many derided it for the criminal identification it brought to the entire Italian culture. They considered idolizing criminals a blatant cultural disrespect. So, who represents the culture?

If one wanted Christianity to represent the actual culture of Jesus' followers, it would have to address the same inconsistencies. Who is in charge and which group is the representative. In my book, *The Jesus You Never Met, Know My Voice V*, I address some of these concerns. Who are the real followers of Jesus? I use the term followers because the term Christian is never used in the bible by Jesus' followers to describe themselves[93]. It is a term used to describe the followers of Jesus by outsiders. This is another translational misrepresentation. The hundreds of denominations and independent organizations that identify as Christian are clueless about this fact, or worse, they ignore it. Additionally, the dogma of these organizations stands in the face of each other. One example is communion. The Roman Catholic, Lutheran, and Evangelical communion are vastly different in definition and procedure. The management of saints is another gulf that exists between the denominations. Because of these and other discrepancies, I don't really see the advantage in identifying as a Christian. To anyone who cares, the word is unidentifiable. But only a few care.

---

[93] Gruber, Daniel; The Separation of Church and Faith, Copernicus and the Jews. Elijah Publishing Hanover 2005 p132

What about those who do care? What are people to do? I understand the dilemma. If one is a follower of The Messiah, Jesus of Nazareth, Christianity is the closest identity that people can comprehend in relation to this central figure. So, everybody remains a Christian.

And few, like me, reject the term and identity due to the ambiguity. Why? The entire group who follows Jesus as The Messiah does have a common thread. To all of us, Jesus is very alive. It is my contention that since he is alive, we need to get our bearings directly from him. And the more foreboding thought is that he sees and knows every thought and action of our life. So, our direction must come from the source Jesus himself predicted would guide us, the Holy Spirit. And that direction is always in the flow of the River of God. We do need another group identification, so to speak. So, then let us consider another direction.

Did you know Jesus of Nazareth had offspring?[94] No, he was not married. No, he did not marry Mary Magdalene. No, his disciples did not take him out of the

---

94 Ibid 36

tomb only being near to death. No, he did not subsequently live a quiet life in seclusion and become a family man. Believe it or not, these are just some of the postulated theories of those who chose not to accept the biblical accounts of the resurrection. Yet, there is a truth. The Messiah, Jesus, did rise from the dead and start a family. This Jesus offers all a spiritual blood line, his Holy Spirit. This Jesus offers membership in the Family of God. This Jesus offers new birth, spiritual birth from God The Father[95]. This family membership represents Jesus' followers, not Christianity. The Family was an idea that became polluted due to the brokenness of humans. Humans turned a family relationship into an organizational diagram. And like the criminals of the Italian culture, there are people who don't represent the family, they are simply part of the organized crime of organized religion. They distort simple teachings such as guidance from the Holy Spirit. Thus, Christianity goes in every which way except toward the King. The Holy Spirit offers a family connection to God. The Holy Spirit offers only one

---

[95] But as many as received Him, to them He gave the right to become children of God, *even* to those who believe in His name, [13] who <u>were born</u> not of blood, nor of the will of the flesh, nor of the will of man, but <u>of God</u>. (Joh 1:12-13 NAS)

direction. This relationship begins the road toward the real Jesus and offers completion for the individual. The Finger of God reaches out to touch the heart and mind of the individual. It is not an easy path because there is no mob urging one on. It is a whisper[96] heard in the wind as it blows by your ear. You will feel alone until you realize you are not alone. Jesus brought the sword, and his family cannot avoid its work. Don't trade off God's invitation for organizational membership.

---

[96] *but* the LORD *was* not in the wind. And after the wind an earthquake, *but* the LORD *was* not in the earthquake. [12] And after the earthquake a fire, *but* the LORD *was* not in the fire; and after the fire a <u>sound of a gentle blowing</u>. [13] And it came about when Elijah heard *it*, that he wrapped his face in his mantle, and went out and stood in the entrance of the cave. And behold, a voice *came* to him and said, "What are you doing here, Elijah?" (1Ki 19:11-13 NAS)

Is Religion in God's Plan

Religion can be a complex proposition. The word religion simply defines a human idea. So does the word gender. Unlike the word gender, which represents something in this realm, the perception of religion relates to the unseen realm and tries to address events that connect our realm with this spiritual realm. Humans have depended on the idea of religion as far back as history is recorded. Humankind innately knows there is a God/deity whose power goes beyond that of their own. So, humankind had to design parameters within which they could understand, relate to, and manage the relationship with this deity. In this process, much religious dogma has come into existence. How did this occur? One way was interaction with the spiritual realm[97] such as mediums, seers, witches, etc. And then there are the four voices that my books detail. The problem is that not all are God's voice. So, religious thought developed and expanded throughout history with these voices. There are now many religions.

---

[97]Then Saul said to his servants, "Seek for me a woman who is a medium, that I may go to her and inquire of her." And his servants said to him, "Behold, there is a woman who is a medium at En-dor." (1Sa 28:7 NAS)

Interestingly, they are all very similar in their goals. They want money and power. Religious thought is born out of superstition. Religious thought attempts to direct and control the actions of people by preying on the human emotion of fear. The Greek word for religion can also be translated as superstition[98]. I find the idea of superstition more closely related to what most people believe in as religion. It is worthwhile to define superstition.

1. An irrational belief that an object, action, or circumstance not logically related to a course of events influences its outcome.
2. A belief, practice, or rite irrationally maintained by ignorance of the laws of nature or by faith in magic or chance.
3. A fearful or abject state of mind resulting from such ignorance or irrationality.[99]

And to define religion:

1. The belief in and reverence for a supernatural power or powers, regarded as creating and governing the universe.
   "respect for religion."

---

[98] 22 Then Paul stood in the midst of Mars' hill, and said, *Ye* men of Athens, I perceive that in all things ye are too <u>superstitious</u>. (Act 17:22 KJV)

[99] The American Heritage® Dictionary of the English Language, 5th Edition •

2. A particular variety of such belief, especially when organized into a system of doctrine and practice.
   "the world's many religions."
3. A set of beliefs, values, and practices based on the teachings of a spiritual leader.[100]

Compare the first bullets of each definition. The only conceptual difference is the word irritational. Most atheists would challenge the religious world with the argument presented in the first bullet of superstition by referencing the first bullet of religion. I am not an atheist, but I do find the idea of superstition to be inextricably intertwined with the religions of today. And I find this interlocking phenomenon primarily the result of the second and third bullets and their relationship. The key is the word fearful. It is fear that paralyzes people from asking questions, digging deeper, and challenging assumed authority. It is fear that drives humans to the ignorance and irrationality of what they believe without the smallest effort of research and critical assessment.

---

[100] The American Heritage® Dictionary of the English Language, 5th Edition •

The religions of the world have confiscated the interpretation and existence of God and the spiritual realm. They define it in a manner that simply fills the vacancies of the human mind and its idle propensities. Humanity sits hour after hour looking at flat-screen information that is manipulated and twisted into words and pictures that feed their brokenness[101]. Religion is just one item on the list. It deceptively fills their sense of security until the moment people really need God. At that point, they realize they have been alone for a long time. I don't want to believe most people think we end up as dirt, but many do. Since this lack of surety is a void, they need to fill that void. They must manufacture another end. Religion fills that void because it is the expert that they are not. The superstition of religion while offering a sense of comfort, creates many more voids than it fills.

As a daily occurrence, the God I espouse is unseen. His realm is also unseen. But I experience God in the same options of my life that humans are presented with

---

[101] For the time will come when they will not endure sound doctrine; but *wanting* to have their ears tickled, they will accumulate for themselves teachers in accordance to their own desires; (2 Ti 4:3 NAS).

every day. Much of humanity is motivated to try every day, to strive every day. Their inner being is driven. For most, the reasons are unknown or fabricated. Humans follow these unknown forces to live their lives, yet never ask the "why" behind the drive. I am saying the "why" exists and it is not found in religion. It is found in the seed that is the breath of God[102] given to each one of us. That life God created we call ourselves. But that existence is incomplete until it connects back to the Echad relationship that first offered them life. This connection is the Holy Spirit. In the end, without the Holy Spirit, the voices of the world and the demonic will be silenced and alone that human will remain.

Religion is superstition. Religion keeps people living in fear. To my point above, people don't fear doing their job or celebrating a birthday party. They do these and other things because of the life drive which exists within them. But if you tell people to critically assess their religion you have a problem. They will debate, argue, ignore, or reject your proposition. Why? They don't want to jeopardize their standing in the next realm.

---

[102] Then the LORD God formed man of dust from the ground, and breathed into his nostrils the breath of life; and man became a living being. (Gen 2:7 NAS)

I would like to make you a proposition. Human beings think. We think immaterial thoughts. We are at a loss as to the source of those thoughts, although my writings address that loss. We follow those thoughts, sometimes resulting in good and other times resulting in trouble. We refer to this as good decision-making or bad decision-making. Here is my proposition, and it is not really mine. God is immaterial, as we understand material. The immaterial of the Holy Spirit desires to connect with the immaterial of your mind. There is no other god or holy book that proposes this option in this manner outside of Jesus' proposal. Religion dictates that a leader directs the people. My proposition is a relational connection that occurs within. But you must choose. If you are not an atheist, if you are one of those people who can accept the idea of religion, who have tried religion, then you know the void which exists due to this superstition. The real God desires to contact you. That part of you which exists with no real proof, your immaterial part. The hand of God is reaching out to you with the Holy Spirit. God's plan is relationship. Only relationships can address human needs. Only you can make this relationship important enough to pursue.

Only the voice of the Holy Spirit can quell the fear and usher you into not being alone all the time. Reach out and shake the Hand of God.

Humankind's Destiny of Death

In the flesh, there is only one road to travel for humanity. I wrote in detail about this process in my previous book, *Life Death, Hope, The Journey To The Next Realm.* We cannot escape this path. In the light of human knowledge and thought, some of us have concluded it is a reasonable path. For some, it is not so reasonable. When the reality of the thought catches up with their consciousness, it causes fear, anger, and resentment. But there is a universal factor for all. The journey is not easy. It is complex due to content and speed. Whatever one's social status, financial status, religious status, or cultural status, it is a road filled with potholes, curves, hills, and downslopes, and in the end it levels all human status. Interestingly enough, in the final analysis, most would not trade off their life for someone else's. And in this age of media, the proof of my analysis is easily made available for us to witness. I recently watched the movie, "*Elvis*". It was heartbreaking on several levels. To see a human being of that level of notoriety, fame, popularity, and success live in the bondage of human brokenness, made me sad and sick of the human condition. What is the human condition?

Without God, it is a condition of bondage, brokenness, sickness, and death. This ugliness may take a while to adhere itself to the individual, but it is always visible in some manner and ultimately, we see it. And we should hope to see it so we can come to hate it! My friend, Dr. James Buirkle wrote a book on hating sickness and pain. It is a good read. I am simply taking it a step further because human sickness and death are not simply defined by the physical. In this respect, we humans travel one road[103]. We should not take it lightly. Human psychology can help but only to a certain degree. We should seek the voice of the Holy Spirit because the road, ultimately, is spiritual.

---

[103] And inasmuch as it is appointed for men to die once and after this *comes* judgment, (Heb 9:27 NAS)

Human Negativity

I love my father and he did many wonderful deeds in his lifetime. But there was one area where he gave in to the voice of the demonic. He was not alone as this trait is very common to humanity, yet most people don't even realize they are being deceived. My mother used to call my father "Eddie no" because if she wanted to visit her family, my father's first response was always "no". Eventually, he came around, but it usually meant a spousal battle of words. When this occurs in a relationship, the demonic beast affecting the relationship is given power and authority. Because of my mom's story, I began to listen to all the times I said "no" to other people, mostly my wife or all the times I had a better method, smarter idea, or more informed opinion. Then I began to hear other people's "NOs" and the rationale behind them. If you stop and begin to listen, the first general response, on an array of topics, from another human is usually negative in some way. We may use the word *no* or we may think it, or we may put forth an opposing argument or opinion. This "no" gene is so prevalent it has become a financial windfall for anyone in the media or on any podcast. We cannot hear it. We cannot see it. We will not believe it. But it is alive and well. Now that you are aware of this demonic intrusion in your life, I suggest you listen and allow the Holy Spirit to point you in another direction. Don't be a naysayer.

The Blind Spot

In my writings, I have referenced my life as a younger man. I was an angry disciplinarian with my children. I was entitled where my wife was concerned, believing it was her responsibility to perform certain chores or have certain attitudes. I was disrespectful toward my parents and siblings. I had a superiority complex in many aspects of my life. I manipulated many situations to my advantage. I taught wrong principles and misled people. None of this behavior benefited me in a real way. My minor success in business and the voices of the demonic and the world kept me living in my make-believe world. I was not respected, but my perceived success kept those around me also living in my make-believe world because they could tag along and, maybe receive some perceived benefit. I could not see it. It was a blind spot.

In my book *He Will Guide You*, I wrote how the Holy Spirit brings up specific memories for our benefit. I read a book in high school. One of the chapters was about the eye's blind spot. The blind spot of the eye is an interesting phenomenon. To demonstrate this experience, the author drew two black figures on either side of the page. The instructions were to cover the right eye with your hand. Next, you were told to look at the figure on the left and slowly scan to the right. About the time you get to the figure on the right the one on the left completely disappears. You can see the entire page, but you cannot see the figure. I have demonstrated this for many people over the years. So, the blind spot is truly a blind "spot". When an object is in that spot you don't realize it cannot be seen. Most people don't even know about their blind spot. Blindness also has to do with recognition. I wrote how it took me thirty years to recognize that the Newark Airport logo was a plane. Have you ever seen the picture that presents the illusion of both a young lady and old lady. Vision and recognition can be tricky. It is like the movie where one character says to the other, "How can you be so sure of what you don't know?" I was!

About the time I began to listen to the voice of the Holy Spirit, I began to be informed by God about my blind spots. First, the voice of the Holy Spirit reminded me of the book I mentioned in the previous paragraph. As I listened, the voice of the Holy Spirit demonstrated my lack of awareness of what was really missing. And since I was so keen at seeing others blind spots, the Holy Spirit turned my vison inward. I was broken, I was ugly, I was evil. I also understood that God's word incorporated judgment. I began to see mine. Any fear I had driving my life became dwarfed by the fear of the Lord as I grew closer to God's reality. The Holy Spirit began to teach me it is better to judge yourself here and now than take your chances before the King. The voice of the Holy Spirit, which I will speak about shortly, is key to this process.

What was most disturbing about this revelation process is my next comment. Having an opinion or seeing a situation in a certain way, for humanity, is mostly a choice. I chose to embrace my brokenness because I thought I could differentiate between good and evil. I could not! We cannot, but we deceive ourselves with our make-believe demarcation of good or evil. I had it backwards. Humanity has it backwards. Good intentions can never overcome bad actions. Now you might say, what about the blind spot, that is not a choice. All of us humans know we make errors, misjudge, and act hastily. We know we have the blind spot, but we use our rationale to misdirect its damage. As humanity spews out anger and hate they rationalize its benefits and ignore its reality. Their make-believe world has them thinking they are doing good or that good intentions will exonerate them. The demonic, the world and the voice of self introduce fear, and we choose fear over change. Good intentions can never overcome evil actions, only Jesus can[104].

As I began to hear more clearly the voice of the Holy Spirit, the Voice encouraged change. All my brokenness, bad habits, and bad attitude mentioned earlier in this chapter became visible. What was more interesting was the reason behind my brokenness. It was fear. My fears, which were incorporated like strands of spaghetti in my life needed to be worked on one strand at a time. It began with relationships with my immediate family. I had to painstakingly pull one strand at a time being careful not to disrupt the entire dish. A person cannot change overnight and most of those we know are also aware of this fact. We all have seen too

---

[104] He was oppressed and afflicted, yet he did not open his mouth; he was led like a lamb to the slaughter, and as a sheep before its shearers is silent, so he did not open his mouth. (Isa 53:7 NIV)

many fox-hole conversions go in reverse. So, it took time for my wife and children to believe I was changing. We also must keep in mind that others' lives are also like spaghetti and when you are a family the entire group is like the dish of spaghetti. Pulling too fast and hard can break strands and cause huge disruptions. So, the process is slow and arduous. This is ok because our human capacity can only take in certain amounts of direction from the Holy Spirit, or we become overloaded. God knows this and so, He works in a way that can benefit all of us at the same time[105].

Fear is not only a personal issue but also a universal problem for humanity. In this country, both political parties have been proven wrong on many issues, but they will not deviate from their prospective platforms. They choose fear over change. The rate of divorce and adultery in our society is rampant because the participants choose fear over change. The media must remain in their political lanes because they choose fear over change. Some of the changes in my life felt, and

---

[105] Ibid 27

feels, like I am ripping out my eye[106]. This change was the result of The King bringing the sword. I didn't like it. I don't like it. But it is necessary for self-judgment. God's right arm is not too short to reach into you and work change. The voice of the Holy Spirit will establish boundaries for you. And when God's finger draws those personal lines in the sand, those demarcations will assist in the process of change. One line has to do with how you treat others. And once you give The Holy Spirit permission, you can expect a range of internal relational interactions from graceful challenges to somber reckonings. Jesus announced the process[107] in this manner. We can throw ourselves onto the Rock or we can have the Rock crush us. Breaking will occur! You just need to decide if you want to judge yourself now or wait until you meet The King.

Humanity has existed in this realm for millennia and has no clue about how to live life. Even when it is right in front of their eyes. And I am not necessarily referring to the bible. Yes, the bible is very relevant but, the voice of the Holy Spirit visits people regularly. They cannot

---

[106] And if your eye causes you to stumble, gouge it out and throw it away. It is better for you to enter life with one eye than to have two eyes and be thrown into the fire of hell. (Mat 18:9 NIV)

[107] Ibid 63

recognize the illusion of the make-believe world, so they cannot hear the voice. The gods of religion, politics, and media interpret, via their representatives, the illusion of this life. An illusion where hate, anger, money, and power rule. The make-believe world that mankind has made and adheres to blinds humanity. And when it cannot be seen the words of the bible, or the voice of the Holy Spirit is muted. Don't let your blind spot blind your need.

The God Humans Created

Most of my writing speaks of the merciful and compassionate voice of the Holy Spirit. But you will also find in my writings that the voice of the Holy Spirit can be challenging, direct, and reckoning if one is ready to receive this guidance. The problem is that the voice of the demonic combined with a broken humanity thwarts the direction of God's plan of relationship with the individual. Too often, humans fail to understand their own personal reckoning needs while at the same time becoming a voice of correction for others. Humanity has no problem giving grace to themselves or those they love while condemning those with whom they disagree. When you disrespect others, any others, you encroach on God's Sovereignty[108]. God cannot vacate His sovereignty. In my journey, I have found that when I consider crossing a line into an area God has marked off, the voice of the Holy Spirit is fast to warn me. I hear, the Voice saying; "are you sure you want to say those words or take that action?" In many ways, humankind

---

[108] But even the archangel Michael, when he was disputing with the devil about the body of Moses, did not himself dare to condemn him for slander but said, "The Lord rebuke you!" (Jud 1:9 NIV)

fails to recognize they have crossed this sovereignty line. Why? God exists. And gods exist. If you are missing the voice of the Holy Spirit, the god you are following is leading you astray. There is no warning for stepping on their sovereignty because you determine their sovereignty. You cannot define the real God in a way that suits your needs. The God of Israel is God. The bible testifies to this truth. The Holy Spirits' voice testifies to this truth. Any other god is a god you have made and most of the time it is the god of self.

The Addiction of Hollywood Dilemma

I love watching movies. I have seen many movies that were entertaining and many that made me feel like I just wasted two hours. You would probably think that I would only watch faith-based movies. But I don't. I now watch movies so I can know what the writer, producers and directors were thinking. I am much more interested in movie messaging than movie content. My best friend's favorite movie is *It's A Wonderful Life.* I could be wrong, but I don't think that at the time it was made it would be considered faith-based. Yet it does make a statement concerning another realm, the spiritual realm. So does the entire genre of Horror movies. Why do I believe we have a problem with movies, television, and media in general. In my first book, I make the point that everything is teaching.

Actors have a special talent to make the audience believe what they see on the screen. Their talent makes what we watch inviting, seductive and, depending on the content, makes emulation desirable. Broken humanity has a propensity to want to reproduce the activity they see, especially if it impresses them. Let us take romantic movies as an example. The ideas, emotions and acts of love and sex have been confiscated by Hollywood and other media formats. When an adolescent begins to inquire about sex, the conversation should include the deep emotional and physical implications of the act of intimacy. But they do not. Add to this the ease of attaining this information from movies, television, books, and the internet, and we have a crisis, a teaching crisis. Consider this; Muslims would not want their young children raised in a Christian household and Christians would not want their young children raised in a Muslim household. This idea probably applies to all religions. So why do we abdicate the teachings of intimacy to those who are morally and ethically disillusioned?

When we combine the story making with the storytelling with the acting out of the story, we can create an indelible mark on the human mind and psyche. The stories, even if not based on real life, guide thought, which guides actions, which produces results. Here are some of those results:

1. We have become numb to violence.

2. The level of hypocritical concepts concerning sex, as taught in many movies is damaging to an already broken human mind.
3. We have become enamored with words that appear to express wisdom.
4. We have been seeded with cultural hate on an obvious level.
5. We have been seeded with cultural hate on a subliminal level.
6. This seedling has added to our anger, fear, and distrust for mostly everyone, especially those who disagree with us.
7. The genre usually does not matter because most people go into a movie that feeds their current needs, ethics, morals, culture, faith, politics, etc.
8. Humans develop many layers over time, even if they try to stay current. The levels that comprise our life get lost over time in this structure blocking our ability to recognize how each of us has arrived at our present state of mind. In other words, we lose track of what really made us into our current selves, a fact directly in our blind spot.

All these results are fed by Hollywood. But we can turn this addictive upside-down teaching to our benefit. Movies, television series, books, and all forms of media should really challenge us to be critical thinkers. As stated earlier, I watch movies, or portions of them, to learn how the source of the movie is attempting to direct or teach me. I don't exclude any input from these sources because it offers me the opportunity, with the Holy Spirit, to evaluate and understand more of how God thinks versus how the world thinks. It is the level of addiction that exploits the human psyche but once revealed and assisted by the Holy Spirit, can be broken and individual healing begins. It happened to me. About eight years ago there was a detective series that caught my attention. I remember watching it. I remember coming home from work intending to watch it. I remember scheduling my day, and my recording unit so I would not miss any episodes. I was addicted. Even their way of drinking coffee made me want to emulate their actions. If it was not for fate, the Holy Spirit, and human brokenness, I may still be watching this series. As it turned out, the series ended abruptly due to the contract of the actor not being renewed. The writers had to put together a poorly written ending for the show. I was disappointed, to say the least. So were many people. The show ran for eight seasons. I began to consider how much time I wasted following this series.

The problem is we don't know what we cannot see. So, the addictions continue. My cold turkey experience made me resolve to never get caught off guard again. The voice of the Holy Spirit can reveal truths that the other voices blind us to because God is attempting to bring people in not exclude them.

The Addiction of Media Dilemma

When I was young, television was young. I remember there were only seven broadcast stations on a black and white screen not much bigger than a computer tablet. And only two channels ran cartoons. My cousin and I disagreed on which station was the best. He watched channel nine and I watched channel eleven. As I write this chapter it is interesting to think that at that age and at that time in history the seeds of addiction were planted and the voices of self, the demonic and the world were already staking out their territory in my mind. Media has grown into the King Kong of psychological beasts. Humanity has been misled since the Garden of Eden. The evidence is well recorded by our history, but the pace of our current deception is staggering. Thousands of streams of series, movies, shopping networks, and news broadcasts lead the way. With the advent of cell phones, we are bombarded moment by moment with teaching disguised as entertainment. Humans can learn how to construct weapons on the internet and employ them in hateful evil acts. This happened on Nine Eleven. God has reached out to slow the pace and reduce the damage, but you must change where you are looking to protect yourself and your family. Humans simply need to look for and believe in this intervention[109] by seeking the voice of the Holy Spirit and rejecting the current teaching of the media.

---

[109] [16] For God so loved the world that he gave his one and only Son, that whoever believes in him shall not perish but have eternal life. (Joh 3:16 NIV)

The Deceptive Addiction of Religion Dilemma

We have discussed two areas that draw humankind away from God and now we can discuss another. The third leg of the stool of deception is religion. The most basic question to ask is what religion, sect, cult, or denomination knows the truth? Which group holds Truth in their grasp and offers it to humankind concerning the realm of God and even the Being of God? They all clearly represent a god. All believe they represent the real God. And all believe their competitors represent false gods. These conclusions are universal, after all, why would you credit the opposition with offering truth! The fundamental piece of information to consider is we are asking the wrong question. Just as in the movie, *It's A Wonderful Life*", George says, "Potter isn't selling, Potter is buying". Religion takes much more than it gives. Organizations cannot offer God to human beings because God is not some wax museum attraction where you get a ticket for entry to view some inanimate figurine. If you buy their tickets, you will get fake lifelessness. No organization can offer relationship between two people, and certainly not with God. They cannot offer the relationship that God requires and imbues. They can only offer situational options, like a religious service and religious observances. God has rejected religion[110]. But you may say to me, "they sure have a lot of people". I will explain this also.

In the process of this offering, three events occur. First, there can arise an emotionally ecstatic feeling that overcomes an individual. It is referred to as the presence of God falling on the person or group. I cannot discount God doing what He wants to do and when He wants to do it, but human emotion is powerful. I have seen this emotional response duplicated in sporting events and concert events. People are enamored with the power of the performer(s). And like the mob that humanity can become, they lose themselves in the emotional awe that the mob creates and attribute this high to an interaction with God. The second type is not so vocal. It is a time of quiet and solitude. The participant spends time in quiet

---

[110] "I hate, I despise your religious festivals; your assemblies are a stench to me. [22] Even though you bring me burnt offerings and grain offerings, I will not accept them. Though you bring choice fellowship offerings, I will have no regard for them. [23] Away with the noise of your songs! I will not listen to the music of your harps. [24] But let justice roll on like a river, righteousness like a never-failing stream! (Amo 5:21-24 NIV)

prayer, with or without music. The amount of time can also vary. It can range from minutes to days. Historically, some have even spent weeks and months in solitude, such as monks. This is not so unlike the concert goer who smokes pot or drinks and when a slow song is performed, they sway and close their eyes and enter a quiet solitude. The third type is a sort of meditation-like event whereby the participants envelop themselves in some type of disciplinary functionality. It generally includes some sort of physical training discipline. Many Eastern practices follow these patterns. One of the claims is a sense of peace. Valium produces the same result. People can be deceived. The religious mob experience brings with it this third addiction. That of religion itself. Religion is a "check off the box" process. If one does all the required processes, they believe they are following the plan God has ordained and this produces favor, God's favor. This addiction is a deception. These organizational processes cannot offer what the Holy Spirit can offer.

God can never be counted out of interacting with humans unless the human rejects the relationship. And no one or thing can replace God in this scenario, God will not have it[111]. To be sure, wherever and whatever people do, God can enter the landscape. My writings are simply to inform you that God probably has come into your reality at various times, attempting to draw you into a relationship, not an organization. The Holy Spirit's presence is one that works like a close friend. The Holy Spirit shows up where you are living, working, or playing. This relationship can be like that of a loved one, such as a parent, sibling, or friend. You don't need to check off boxes to potentiate this relationship. You simply need to invite the Holy Spirit into yourself, your living home. One simply needs to act in the manner that the relationship dictates. This relationship is reciprocal, with the human receiving most, if not all, the benefit, of True companionship. All my other writings disseminate some of these possible dictates of the relationship. This is why reading my books can help you. God has requirements. If you allow them to be filtered by organizational religion, you will miss the best God has for you. Invite the Holy Spirit in and meet God in your house. His arm is always reaching out.

---

[111] You shall not bow down to them or worship them; for I, the LORD your God, am a jealous God, (Exo 20:5 NIV)

The Line in The Sand

The finger of God has appeared in human history. The biblical event was recorded in the book of Daniel[112]. God thought this was such a significant time in human history that His finger wrote a message on a cement wall. That night human history shifted.

God allows everything that occurs in human society, but keep in mind allowing is different than agreeing. Sometimes God is behind an occurrence for some reason. Other times God simply allows another source to act. We see this in the book of Job. Historically, various nations and governments have been granted the authority and power to conquer and rule. God granted Nebuchadnezzar to rule for a time. God allowed Alexander the Great to rule for a time. God allowed Rome to rule for a time. Interestingly all these historical events are found in the book of Daniel[113]. The same book where we see God's finger.

---

[112] Ibid 22

[113] "After you, another kingdom will arise, inferior to yours. Next, a third kingdom, one of bronze, will rule over the whole earth. [40] Finally, there will be a fourth kingdom, strong as iron--for iron breaks and smashes everything--and as iron breaks things to pieces, so it will crush and break all the others. (Dan 2:39-40 NIV)

My next comment may make many people unhappy. All worldwide events which feed human history relate to and are a result of God's relationship with Israel. They are not a result of His relationship with religious organizations, Christianity, or any other nation. As stated earlier, though there may be people within these groups that will fall under the umbrella of The Israel of God, it is National Israel that is driving human history. This recent war with Hamas has the entire world involved. Let me say it another way. These other groups may appear to have an effect, or take a priority, but it is only a byproduct of the first relationship. People protest Israel every day. Israel is front page every day. Where are the Ukraine-Russia protesters? That war has been muted and accepted, and the vicarious term *genocide* is rarely mentioned. This is not the case with Israel and Hamas. In an earlier chapter, I address Israel. Their country is about as big as the state of New Jersey, yet they influence entire cultures, nations, and religions when it comes to the plan of God. The fact that they have been and are hated is a matter of great significance. The amount of attention that Israel draws is a result of their status with God. If you look at the

UN, Israel has no status! But where God is concerned, Israel is paramount. Not that they are more loved by God but simply because they are loved[114]. Abraham, Isaac, Jacob, and Jesus, through love, accepted The Father's sovereignty. God's sovereignty is the hinge on which the rest of us turn.

Like Israel, the human scenario is more about God's love for us. But all do not love God. Even in Israel all do not love God but their existence is intricately intertwined in God's plan for humanity. Jesus, The Messiah, The King of Israel is the heart of the plan. God is beyond understanding but the parts we can understand tell us he does not consider one person more valuable than another[115]. So how does Israel, The Chosen People play into humanity. As I mentioned previously, there is nothing that humankind can supply, universally speaking, to God that God does not have already. What God desires is the intimate relationship of the individual human. Because of whom

---

[114] "I have loved you," says the LORD. "But you ask, 'How have you loved us?'"Was not Esau Jacob's brother?" declares the LORD. "Yet I have loved Jacob, (Mal 1:2 NIV)

[115] Then Peter began to speak: "I now realize how true it is that God does not show favoritism [35] but accepts from every nation the one who fears him and does what is right. (Act 10:34-35 NIV)

God is, this has huge benefits for the individual. Much of humankind still rejects the voice of the Holy Spirit. But long ago, God chose one man, and consequently, one group, with which to interact. Many of those interactions are recorded in the bible. The specific interaction that made Israel the Chosen People was with a man whom God referred to as a friend. His name was Abraham. The interaction was a simple one. God was so moved by this man that He gave Abraham a promise. Abraham would become a community of Nations.[116] and there would be good for anyone who blessed Abraham's lineage and there would be trouble for all who mistreat/curse this nation. The Nation is Israel and the community it represents. Showing respect for Israel shows respect for God because Israel was God's choice. When God makes a choice, it should be honored first because of relationship, friendship, love, and mostly because of sovereignty. Several biblical personalities demonstrated this principle. Most notable was King David[117] when he would not harm King Saul because King Saul was God's anointed. King Saul was a bad King

---

[116] Ibid 5

[117] 6 He said to his men, "The LORD forbid that I should do such a thing to my master, the LORD's anointed, or lay my hand on him; for he is the anointed of the LORD." (1Sa 24:6 NIV)

yet; he was proclaimed King by God through Samuel the Prophet. He was God's choice and David honored God's sovereignty. The principle is also communicated to us with the events of Moses' life. Egypt's King failed to acknowledge and respect Israel, so God brought judgment upon them[118]. On the other side of this principle was King Nebuchadnezzar who when finally acknowledging God as sovereign was released from the madness that he experienced[119]. These last two examples are what the nations/gentiles reap when standing against the sovereignty of God. The nations are not fighting Israel, they are fighting God's sovereignty, a battle that cannot be won. I refer to this as the gentile side of the Chosen People equation. But there is more.

There is an Israel side of the Chosen People equation. Repeatedly God held the people of Israel responsible for not participating in the relationship. For following other

---

[118] Now the LORD had said to Moses, "I will bring one more plague on Pharaoh and on Egypt. After that, he will let you go from here, (Exo 11:1 NIV)

[119] At the same time that my sanity was restored, my honor and splendor were returned to me for the glory of my kingdom. My advisers and nobles sought me out, and I was restored to my throne and became even greater than before. 37 Now I, Nebuchadnezzar, praise and exalt and glorify the King of heaven, because everything he does is right and all his ways are just. And those who walk in pride he is able to humble. (Dan 4:36-37 NIV)

gods. Yet there are two concepts that non-Jews must keep in mind about Israel. First and foremost is there are Jewish people who recognize God's plan concerning the Messiah, who recognize Yeshua (Jesus) as that Messiah and are witnesses to that plan. There are many Jews who do this already but, Israel at large has not. The second is to consider the way Jews embrace their Jewishness. I once heard a messianic Jewish teacher say that there is something in the genes of Jewish people that draws them to their Jewishness, another result of God's sovereignty. I get his analogy and realize that this is the continued participation of Jews in the Chosen People equation. The Call goes deeper than flesh but freewill can resist the voice of the Holy Spirit. Israel, as a nation, validates God and His actions over the millennia. Gentiles need to seriously consider these events. But the bible also indicates God requires more from the Jewish people. Jewish people expressing Jewishness is Jewish-centric. Jewish people adhering to their God is God-centric, God requires the God-centric part also. Why? Not because God is selfish but because it will benefit them. Choosing God benefits all who choose Him. The Father sent Jesus of Nazareth to express this God-centric philosophy by demonstrating it as a Jew. This demonstration culminated in his resurrection from the dead, being confirmed as Messiah and being crowned King of the Jews, and King of the universe. Jesus offers Citizenship into Israel's community[120] to people of all nations, cultures, and families because it is the fulfillment of the promise to Abraham.

All of what I am speaking of is the arm of God reaching into this realm and is the finger of God drawing a line in the sand. That line is Israel. If you join the King of the Jews, Jesus the Messiah, you will respect that line and you will become God-centric and become part of God's Chosen People equation. There will be many blessings but there is also a personal reckoning for anyone who enters this relationship. The voice of the Holy Spirit will not only validate this truth but will help you experience *Echad* relationship[121]. That Voice will also reveal what is required[122] of you by God. If you

---

[120] Ibid 5

[121] I have given them the glory that you gave me, that they may be one as we are one-- 23 I in them and you in me--so that they may be brought to complete unity. (Joh 17:22-23 NI

[122] 10 "So you too, when you do all the things which are commanded you, say, 'We are unworthy servants; we have done that which was required of us.'" (Luk 17:10 NAS)

decide to be religion-centric, culture-centric, or nation-centric, you will miss the Holy Spirit's voice.

The Messiah and Authority

Have you ever been in a courtroom, I mean a higher courtroom? I know someone who was accused and tried in the federal court. When I attended the trial, as I entered the courtroom, I could sense the authority that resided in that place, and it wasn't necessarily good, but it was authority. Many judgments are made in that room and the principalities[123] and powers of the demonic stand ready to affect these proceedings. It was both awe-full and awful. That was an earthly taste of the reality of the principle of judgment. That empty room was filled with unseen powers whose mere presence invited fear. It was a spiritual thing, not a physical thing. I could not help, that day in the courtroom, contemplating the power and the authority of God. God's authority is beyond comprehension. It can be introduced cognitively by the biblical term, "the fear of the Lord" but it can only be apprehended by an encounter with Truth. As I wrote in my book, *He Will Guide You,* Truth is not a thought, it is not data, it is an

---

[123] [12] For our struggle is not against flesh and blood, but against the rulers, against the authorities, against the powers of this dark world and against the spiritual forces of evil in the heavenly realms. (Eph 6:12 NIV)

experience, an encounter with God. I know this first-hand from several personal reckoning encounters with the Holy Spirit. Just the presence of God overwhelms the human inner being and is experienced by the physical body.

The next to last chapter of this book speaks to our final reckoning with The King. I wrote an entire book on *The Jesus You Never Met*. Reading that book can be the beginning for someone to learn about a Jesus not offered by religion. The religious community has defined Jesus to the point where only certain bible verses are used to discover his personality. But there are other verses that also demonstrate his personality. My focus is on two events recorded after the resurrection where the Apostle John met Jesus. The first is before his ascension to heaven and the second is after.

When John and the other disciples met Jesus that day on the beach of the Sea of Galilee, John said something that I found very interesting. John, and the others, were afraid to ask if it was really Jesus[124]. He clearly was unrecognizable as the Jesus known to John

---

[124] 2 Jesus said to them, "Come and have breakfast." None of the disciples dared ask him, "Who are you?" They knew it was the Lord. (Joh 21:12 NIV)

and the other disciples, while at the same time being the risen Jesus. Jesus had a mission to accomplish here on earth. He completed that mission. While he is loving, compassionate, and merciful, Jesus also recognizes the seriously broken state that is humankind. He endured tremendous suffering to bring us back into his Father's Kingdom. During his ministry, Jesus communicated often to his disciples in ways that confounded and confronted them[125]. Jesus was serious about the redemption of humankind, and he wanted his disciples to be serious also. Psalm 2[126] is a view into this seriousness. John and the other disciples understood this about The Messiah, hence their fear that day on the beach. The relationship between two people is deep waters. By allowing the Holy Spirit to bring honest

---

[125] [37] They replied, "Let one of us sit at your right and the other at your left in your glory." [38] "You don't know what you are asking," Jesus said. "Can you drink the cup I drink or be baptized with the baptism I am baptized with?" (Mar 10:37-38 NIV).

[126] **Psalm 2:1** Why do the nations conspire and the peoples plot in vain? [2] The kings of the earth rise up and the rulers band together against the LORD and against his anointed, saying, [3] "Let us break their chains and throw off their shackles." [4] The One enthroned in heaven laughs; the Lord scoffs at them. [5] He rebukes them in his anger and terrifies them in his wrath, saying, [6] "I have installed my king on Zion, my holy mountain." [7] I will proclaim the LORD's decree: He said to me, "You are my son; today I have become your father. [8] Ask me, and I will make the nations your inheritance, the ends of the earth your possession. [9] You will break them with a rod of iron; you will dash them to pieces like pottery." [10] Therefore, you kings, be wise; be warned, you rulers of the earth. [11] Serve the LORD with fear and celebrate his rule with trembling. [12] Kiss his son, or he will be angry and your way will lead to your destruction, for his wrath can flare up in a moment. Blessed are all who take refuge in him. (Psa 2:1-12 NIV)

reckonings into your life will offer a deeper relationship with The King.

Unfortunately, the general attitude of the world we live in today is arrogance. They refuse to be required by anyone to do anything unless it feeds their ego and their bank account. They will follow the voices of the demonic to achieve these ends. And they will exchange the Holy Spirit-led compassion and mercy for the demonic-led anger and hate. These attitudes will not cut it with The King. John and the other disciples experienced this seriousness surrounding the mission of The Messiah. His sacrifice will not be in vain.

After the ascension of Jesus to heaven, John encounters his Messiah once again. Just the physical appearance of Jesus by a human in this realm is too much to even stay on one's feet[127]. There is a dread when encountering The Messiah because there is a reckoning in His Presence. A negative result of that reckoning could be separation from God forever. God did not want this to occur. God does not want this to

---

[127] 17 When I saw him, I fell at his feet as though dead. Then he placed his right hand on me and said: "Do not be afraid. I am the First and the Last. (Rev 1:17 NIV)

occur. But humankind cares little for what God has to say. If I were wrong, the voice of the Holy Spirit would prevail in the minds and actions of the masses. Compassion and mercy would be our standard and we would fly that flag high. This is not the case. Learn this fact now; Truth is an experience, an encounter. The Messiah is Truth.

I Am Who I Am

There is truth to be found in this life. We may not see it. We may not understand it. We may not agree with it. We may not like it but, it can be found. I find myself often noticing talking heads on television make claims of the truth. Many of them say, "the truth is.... blah blah blah." What floored me was the arrogance of the many talking heads who claim to know the truth. Where can truth be found? Where is the truth hiding? Or is truth on display for all to see and share? How can there be competing truths? When I look up the word truth the dictionary conjoins it to the word fact. Is truth represented by fact? In the human mind, there should be a relationship between fact and truth, but this is not so. The problem for humanity is that facts should be based on real occurrences, but they are not because the make-believe world makes up make-believe facts. They are more like accusations being claimed as facts. Once again, I am burdened to see broken humanity not able to recognize truth[128].

---

[128] Ibid 7

I want to speak about the burning bush and Moses. Is this record truth? Does it record facts? Or do you need an audio-visual recording to establish the truth of this event? Bible believers would say that this bible event records fact. My question is, "what exactly is the fact that it records?" Let us take a solemn and contrite moment as we attempt to stand in the presence of Truth. There may be more than one about this encounter, but the overarching fact is that God makes an introduction of Himself into this realm in a way not previously done. We know that God walked with Adam and Eve in the Garden of Eden. We know God called Noah. We know God spoke to Abraham and wrestled with Jacob. We know God gave Joseph dreams. But in this event, this introduction, in this interaction God defines His Being, God's _Echad_ Being! And as He does it, He instructs Moses to remove his shoes because the very ground is Holy. This _Echad_ Being defines eternal existence by defining Its' eternal existence. The statement "I Am" in Hebrew, and maybe in all languages, defines an existence that does not establish a beginning or an end in relation to something else. And in relation to something else, such as time, God is the Beginning and the End. The verse states: "Tell the

Israelites that <u>I AM</u> sent you." In the book of Genesis, God's *Echad* Being is again defined as The Spirit of God hovering over the waters[129]. Millennia later when the Apostle John encounters the risen Messiah, Jesus announces Himself as the beginning and the end. This not only reinforces the statements to Moses and in Genesis, but further helps our understanding of the *Echad* Being, the Unity of God. God is *Echad*, God is a Unity[130]. There is a book by Watchman Nee that offers an interesting look into the *Echad* Being of God, specifically chapter five[131]. It is worth reading.

Why is this chapter important to this writing? Because time, events, people, and the entirety of creation did not exist before God. Nothing can exist without God. Everything exists within God. God owns and orders everything. God established the universe and humanity. God reached out to humanity. God chose Jacob making Israel the Chosen People. God came in the flesh as Jesus of Nazareth, The Messiah, to

---

[129] Now the earth was formless and empty, darkness was over the surface of the deep, and the Spirit of God was hovering over the waters. (Gen 1:2 NIV)

[130] Kaplan, Aryeh. *Maimonides' Principles.* The Fundamentals of Jewish Faith. New York: National Conference of Synagogue, 1975.

[131] Nee, Watchman; Spiritual Authority, Christian Fellowship Publisher Inc. , 1972 p47

reach out to a broken people, to establish The Father's authority and the principles of obedience and sovereignty. The Father and the Son send the Holy Spirit to offer their relationship to broken people. The message of the bible establishes that there will be an end to this process because people choose to follow brokenness instead of Life[132]. The process must end because God declares it so. The end of the process will occur according to God's words, not humanity's brokenness. What can we do about it? Call on the Holy Spirit. Listen for God's voice and direction in ordering your thoughts, life, and actions. The Holy Spirit will guide you if you choose. And you will make it into the Kingdom of Eternal Security. The Kingdom of the *Echad* Being.

---

[132] The rest of mankind who were not killed by these plagues still did not repent of the work of their hands; they did not stop worshiping demons, and idols of gold, silver, bronze, stone and wood--idols that cannot see or hear or walk. [21] Nor did they repent of their murders, their magic arts, their sexual immorality or their thefts. (Rev 9:20-21 NIV)?

The Destiny of Humankind

Humankind has a couple of destinies that they cannot avoid, which I will get to later in the chapter. All the bloviating and word manipulations employed by the talking-heads who speak for the various segments of human politics, religion, sociology, finance, history, and culture cannot change the outcome. These talkers cannot rationalize the "have-nots" side of human brokenness to be the result of bad treatment, lack of education, lack of opportunity, lack of finances, oppression, or just bad luck. These talkers cannot justify the "haves" side of brokenness which perpetrated, and continues to perpetrate, the mistreatment of the "have-nots" by the social, cultural, religious, financial, political, and academic hierarchy. The talking heads will lie, rationalize, and defend themselves. But God sees beyond the beyond. What I mean by beyond the beyond is a simple example once brought to light by a professor of mine. I was attending a class in the 1990s. He asked each of us if we were alive during World War II and living in Nazi Germany, what side would we have taken? Most, if not all, would have liked to think they would have joined the ranks of that current-day Ann Franke's. The professor cautioned the optimism given the challenge of the situation. Some said how could we know? Then the professor said, "but God knows!" God sees beyond the beyond.

The two destinies we cannot avoid are death and standing before The King, Jesus of Nazareth. Upon our arrival, we will know if our life was God-centered or not. We will become acutely aware that the following list is true and accurate.

Your:
1. Religion cannot help you.
2. Money cannot help you.
3. Social status cannot help you.
4. Philosophy cannot help you.
5. Academia cannot help you.
6. Poverty cannot help you.
7. Intelligence cannot help you.
8. Perceived greatness cannot help you.
9. Celebrity cannot help you.
10. Perceived authority cannot help you.
11. Charity cannot help you.

What a farmer plants in a field is what grows[133]. In this life attention to the voice and the direction of the Holy Spirit is paramount. You should critically examine what you have planted, what is growing, and maybe what you should be planting. Work in your field. It is important to your destiny.

---

[133] Do not be deceived: God cannot be mocked. A man reaps what he sows. [8] Whoever sows to please their flesh, from the flesh will reap destruction; whoever sows to please the Spirit, from the Spirit will reap eternal life. (Gal 6:7-8 NIV)

The Only Conduit

The only conduit to an eternity with God is finding and adhering to the voice of the Holy Spirit. The Holy Spirit points us to Jesus, and Jesus connects us to The Father. This is not difficult. It is not about joining a religion. It is about your willingness to contemplate your attitude. God has allowed humanity to arrive at the precipice of universal information availability. This is not new; it just means we have more ways to hear and believe our own rhetoric[134]. The voice of the world and the voice of the demonic are loud and clear. They can overwhelm the voice of self and the Holy Spirit. Just take one look around. We see anger, hatred, and the struggle for power consuming humanity. Humans want to determine what is good and what is evil. Humans want to be the final determiner of what is right and what is wrong. Humans want sovereignty. And boy do they try to get it! It occurs all day at the expense of other humans. Humans cannot recognize broken society is not a cause, movement, institution, company, or

---

[134] Then they said, "Come, let us build ourselves a city, with a tower that reaches to the heavens, so that we may make a name for ourselves; otherwise we will be scattered over the face of the whole earth." (Gen 11:4 NIV)

government but there are people on the other side. And when the losers are finally crushed the winners cheer, gloat, and pump a fist in victory, it is a victory that crushed other human beings. Their rationale: we prevented evil, we have good intentions.

The only voice that can turn us to a godly path is the voice of the Holy Spirit. The Holy Spirit gets us through the distractions of self, the world, and the demonic. This Voice teaches us mercy, compassion, and kindness. This Voice teaches us selflessness in the face of our lowly and mundane lives. This voice teaches us the Holy Spirit is the one conduit to The King Jesus and The King is the one conduit to The Father[135].

---

[135] Jesus answered, "I am the way and the truth and the life. No one comes to the Father except through me. (Joh 14:6 NIV)

The Destiny of The Citizen

The destiny of The Citizen of The Kingdom of God has already been determined in God. Where it has not been determined is in the individual living human being. Now before you get all hot and bothered because of the box created in one's mind concerning Christianity and religion, slow down, get a cup of coffee and listen to the rules that do exist concerning this process. Christianity and religion have muzzled the real message behind the Messiah and the bible. I spoke about this corruption in a previous chapter. So, before putting my writing into some box please consider my entire message. I have referenced the scripture where Jesus says not all who call him Lord will be citizens. This is important to figure out, especially if you are a Christian. But let's say you are not. Where do you stand if you believe the following:

1. There is life after death.

2. There is another realm.

3. God does exist.

4. You cannot accept the idea of hell.

5. You cannot accept the tenets of Christianity as they have been explained to you or as you understand them.

6. You cannot accept any religion as it has been presented to you.

7. You cannot change your religion.

8. Being, in your definition, a good person is enough to get you some reward for this life.

9. Your anger and frustrations are not sins; they are generally sourced in good intentions.

10. If there is a God, He cannot condemn people just because they belong to the wrong religion.

11. (Write your own reason)

This list probably contains a little of everything that goes through the minds of people when they contemplate transition out of this realm. Humans also may hope the list contains information that is considered in God's decision-making process. So how do you sieve out what needs to be removed or what is relevant?

God has given each person what they need to make a successful transition to the next realm. As mentioned in a previous chapter, God expresses hope in our ability to overcome[136] our brokenness. So, it is up to you to find God. God has already found you and has made

---

[136] Ibid 33

Himself known in some fashion. The bible records some of the most stubborn religious people changing. It is not an easy journey. It is filled with bumps and potholes. You will be rejected, maybe even by people who you love or claim they love you. But if you find The Creator, you will find you are not alone. The voice of the Holy Spirit will become your companion, guide, counselor, and mentor. But it is up to you. Rationale cannot help you. Religion cannot help you. Don't leave your destiny in the hands of a human organization. Your destiny lies with God, but you must seek, find, and choose The King. He has reached out.

Reckoning

Why is it important to familiarize yourself with the bible and to work on hearing the voice of the Holy Spirit? Everyone departs this realm. When this occurs, we will be responsible for our decisions, our choices, our life, and our entire self. Contact with God presents the voice of reality and truth. Your entire self will meet Truth! Let me share a story concerning reality, truth and reckoning. My son Joseph joined the Marines. He had a friend who also joined at the same time. As the father of a non-military family, I did not want him to join because of the dangers associated with military service but I eventually gave in to both Joseph's and God's sovereignty. A few years after he joined, he was home on-leave and his friend visited. This friend and I were sitting in the yard having a coffee early one morning. Just out of curiosity, I asked this young man the reckoning question. I said, "When was the moment you realized there was a difference between what you thought military service was prior to your enlisting and what became reality when actually serving?" Reckoning is all about an encounter coming face-to-face with a thought. This is why faith is so important. This young man gave this reply. When he was stationed in Afghanistan his unit was guarding a wedding for a town official. To make a long story short, a car bomb exploded but it never made it onto the wedding grounds. It was close enough to send this young man and his friend flying. After regaining consciousness, the first thing he did was look for his friend. For him that was the moment of reckoning. Fortunately, they both were ok, but I will add this young man also lost his brother in that war. There is no value high enough that I can place on those who honorably serve in the military. Unfortunately, there are also many challenging consequences resulting from this service.

What happens when we die? Before we die, death is simply a thought. If you see death the way I do, thought meets encounter, reckoning! But there are other opinions. Does human demise end with nothingness? Does death result in becoming part of the environment as the body decays and, ultimately, makes us minerals found in the dirt? Is our consciousness only connected to our body? Does our resultant decay after death cause that which we understand as "us" to end? Those who believe these thoughts are known as atheists. If this is your conclusion, and there are many people who have come to this conclusion, it is much sadder than the sadness, or preposterousness of life after death. Without the belief in life after death, this is the end to which we are consigned. With the Holy Spirit, we are presented with options other than our thoughts, our dreams, our ambitions, our accomplishments, our relationships, our hopes, our efforts, our aspirations, our life, the very essence of what we are being consigned to the waste dump of mother earth and disappearing with no record or memory of our existence. While religion is not the answer either, it does open the door to the next realm, but the door is problematic, to say the least. The reason is because there is a gulf between religious thought and biblical facts. I have said enough about this chasm for you to understand my position. Yet this chapter is a message about our reckoning with God. At the point of transition our thoughts will encounter reality, another reality with which we are not familiar. And when that occurs, like my son's friend, when we awaken to the spiritual, we will want to look for our friend. Let it be Jesus. Make The Messiah your friend now and let that relationship be facilitated by the Holy Spirit. It will all be worth it.

Sovereignty

Sovereignty is a subject intricately intertwined with reckoning. Reckoning is a natural result of the phenomenon of sovereignty. It is where the moveable object of creation meets existence, life, reality, and the unchanging nature of God. If you believe in God, in the way the bible presents God, then you must face the issue that God is sovereign. Before I get into some of the more complex topics, the simplest example of God's sovereignty is the fact of human death. In Genesis, God told Adam and Eve they would die if they ate the fruit from the Tree of the Knowledge of Good and Evil. The result? Humankind dies. Humankind since then has died, other than two individuals, Enoch[137] and Elijah[138]. There is nothing humanity can do to avoid, evade, or overturn this fact. The reckoning of human death is the meeting of the sovereign unchanging nature of God and individuals' reality. Even Jesus the Messiah died. His death was all about sovereignty[139] and so was his

---

[137] 24 And Enoch walked with God; and he was not, for God took him. (Gen 5:24 NAS)

[138] 11 Then it came about as they were going along and talking, that behold, *there appeared* a chariot of fire and horses of fire which separated the two of them. And Elijah went up by a whirlwind to heaven (2Ki 2:11 NAS)

[139] Ibid 36

resurrection from the dead. I will get back to Jesus but first I want to speak about the Echad Being of God and the resulting sovereign outcomes.

Everything exists because of God. Everything exists in God[140]. Existing in God is like existing in a house. Typically, parents own the home in which their children live. When my children arose on a Saturday morning, they had two needs: hunger and video games. If they wanted cereal it had to be in the house, it had to exist in the house. If they wanted to play a video game, they needed electricity. It had to be available. It had to exist in the house. This is similar with existing in God. Existing in God yields some interesting results. Everything humans do and everything humans are is only because it exists in the house, in God. Without God, humans can't think, eat, walk, and exist. Without God, there is no cereal or electricity. And it is not because God bought the cereal or electricity. God is the cereal and electricity. Jesus said, "My flesh is real food". I, and others, take it as a metaphor for teaching and others interpret it as the bread of communion becoming

---

[140] 17 And He is before all things, and in Him all things hold together. (Col 1:17 NAS)

God, but he was speaking a deep spiritual truth[141]. God is the food of our existence. God is the house of our occupancy. But God is so much more. Take the concept of unity, agreement, or contract. The fact of two, or more, individuals being subject to a performance agreement is not a trite situation. It should not be taken lightly. One example in human society is marriage agreement. Humans have been promising for millennia to take care of each other and remain with each other until death separates them. As I became more familiar with the Holy Spirit's voice, I became more aware of the universal principles that exist within God. In other words, they exist because of God, not because God made them but because God exists in this manner. God is the principle behind contract, agreement, and unity because God is _Echad_. Let me attempt to offer another example. In the United States, the Constitution is the principal operating foundation. Now the Constitution did not make itself. Yet, due to its self-content the country operates according to this rule. I am not referring to the interpretation of its content but the simple fact of its content. We have lawyers and judges

---

[141] The Spirit gives life; the flesh counts for nothing. The words I have spoken to you-- they are full of the Spirit and life. (Joh 6:63 NIV)

making billions of dollars arguing over its interpretation, but they are doing such according to its content most of the time. It is a self-contained unchangeable result of its existence, for now. This principle comes from God's sovereignty. The contract law concept of marriage, unity, and agreement exists in God and cannot be changed because God's nature does not change[142]. The existence of The Father, the Son, and the Holy Spirit are this unity concept. Hence the term God uses to describe His Being, _Echad_.

In an earlier chapter, I referenced humankind's wiggle room concerning broken agreements. For the purposes of this realm and God's grace God allowed, and allows, wiggle room. If God did not, no one could attain eternal security. But in Jesus the Messiah the very high price for this wiggle room was paid. Sovereignty created humankind, it guides humankind, it supports humankind, it redeemed humankind, it offers eternal security to humankind, and it will judge humankind. Everything exists in God. God is sovereign. Therefore, sovereignty is a critical issue.

---

[142] 17 Because God wanted to make the unchanging nature of his purpose very clear to the heirs of what was promised, he confirmed it with an oath. (Heb 6:17 NIV)

Here is another example of the Sovereignty of God: We have life. We know we have life because society for millennia has agreed on this fact. We value that life. Even pro-choice people value life. They may not value all life, but they value their life and the lives of those they love. Life has meaning. By biblical definition God is Life[143]. And from the same source life was ordained for humanity[144]. Humanity can do little to stop the process of physical life. War has occurred throughout history, but it has never wiped out all humanity. Biblical families that existed millennia ago are gone, except for Israel. But there are still more people than ever. Sovereignty is why physical life goes on. Sovereignty ordained the resurrection of Jesus. Life cannot be extinguished because God cannot be extinguished. The human being's life will go on eternally. All will rise from the dead[145] to be judged. The state of that individual is what is in question.

---

[143] That which was from the beginning, which we have heard, which we have seen with our eyes, which we have looked at and our hands have touched--this we proclaim concerning the Word of life. ² **The life** appeared; we have seen it and testify to it, and we proclaim to you the eternal life, which was with the Father and has appeared to us. (IJo 1:1-2 NIV)

[144] Ibid 99

[145] Rev 20

The next time you think about the following list, consider the implications God's Sovereignty has for your participation in your life, your requirements:

1. Marriage relationship.
2. Parenting relationship.
3. Friendship relationship.
4. Neighbor relationship.
5. Work relationships.
6. Play relationships.
7. Family relationships.

We cannot escape the reality of our participation in human society. It has requirements[146]. These requirements are not optional. They are not situation-dependent. They cannot be altered or changed because they exist just as God exists. The voice of the Holy Spirit will teach you about God's Sovereignty. The Holy Spirit will guide you down this road, helping you see the potholes and helping you avoid them. If you hit some, and you will, the grace of the cross accomplished by The King can help you. Jesus has overcome death and now The King, a human King, rules over death. And at some

---

[146] He has told you, O man, what is good; And what does the LORD require of you But to do justice, to love kindness, And to walk humbly with your God? (Mic 6:8 NAS)

point, this victory will be seen by all the universe and all The Citizens will share in Jesus' victory. For now, we must wait. We must learn. We must grow. Our victory resides in God.

More Info: www.thehouseofbread.com

John's Books

He Will Guide You
Truth, Experience the Holy Spirit

Know My Voice I
The Mystery of the Thread of Israel

Know My Voice II
God Has a Kingdom and it is not Organized Religion

Know My Voice III
The Insanity of Humanity

Know My Voice IV
Marriage, Commitment, Responsibility, Relationship, Intimacy, Choice

Know My Voice V
The Jesus You Never Met

Know My Voice VI
Life, Death, Hope
The Journey to the Next Realm

Know My Voice VII
The King, The Kingdom, The Citizens
Recognizing and Entering The Kingdom

Know My Voice VIII
Christianity, Religion, Deception
The Process of Recognizing, Choosing and Obeying